MARRIAGES AND DEATHS, ACCIDENTS, DUELS AND RUNAWAYS, ETC., COMPILED FROM

THE WEEKLY GEORGIA TELEGRAPH

MACON, GEORGIA
1850-1853

R. NEWTON WILCOX

HERITAGE BOOKS, INC.

HERITAGE BOOKS

AN IMPRINT OF HERITAGE BOOKS, INC.

W2162-A4084HB

Books, CDs, and more – Worldwide

For our listing of thousands of titles see our websites
at
www.WillowBendBooks.com
and
www.HeritageBooks.com

Published 2003 by
HERITAGE BOOKS, INC.

COPYRIGHT
R. NEWTON WILCOX
2002

International Standard Book Number: 0-7884-2162-X

TABLE OF CONTENTS

Issue of Jan 1, 1850

Runaway – from the subscriber, a negro boy named LAWRENCE, about 25 years of age, bright ginger cake color, straight black hair, black eyes, about 5 feet 6 inches high. Said boy left Fort Valley on the 22d, and when last heard from was on the road to Knoxville, enquiring for a Tobacco wagon. A liberal reward will be paid for said boy, on this delivery to the subscriber in Macon county.

NATHAN BRYAN

Issue of Jan 8, 1850

$10 Reward – A reward of Ten Dollars will be paid for the discovery of the ruffians who attacked me on the night of the 19th inst. with knives and pistols, on the road between Walnut Creek Bridge and East Macon.

RICHARD DESHZO

Married – In this city, on the 27th ult. by Rev. W. R. BRANHAM, MR. JNO. C. RIDDLE to MRS. CHRISTIAN ALEXANDER.

On the same evening, by Rev. MR. BRANHAM, MR. JNO. T. CHAPMAN, to MRS. ANN E. CAMPBELL.

In Vineville, on the evening of the 2d inst. By the Rev. MR. ELLISON, Capt. CHARLES A. HAMILTON, of Cass to MISS MADALINE M., daughter of WM. SCOTT, Esq.

Issue of Jan 15, 1850

Stop the Runaway – Runaway from the subscriber, on the 1st inst. his negro man, named NELSON, about 24 years of age, five feet 6 or 8 inches high, complexion quite black, some upper front teeth out, and the others considerably decayed; he is of medium size and weight and somewhat

1

bowlegged. I will give ten dollars reward to any person bringing said man to me, or lodging him in jail, so that I can get him.

Websterville, Bibb county
PETER NEWELL

$500 Reward – The subscribers offer the above Reward for the discovery of the Murderer or Murderers of their deceased brother, JOHN G. PONDER. The murder was perpetrated in Pulaski county, near ten mile creek, on Sunday night, 21st day of October last.

WM. G. PONDER
E.G. PONDER
JAMES PONDER

Issue of Jan 22, 1850

Runaway – On the 4th inst, SARAH, a bright mulatto, about 18 years of age, and about 5 feet high, she has light grey eyes and is quite intelligent, and has lost one of her upper front teeth. Any person who will arrest and deliver her to me, or confine her in jail so that I can get her again, will be liberally rewarded.

Wallace, P.O. Jones County
BENJ. F. FINNEY

Married – In this city, on the 8th inst, by the Rev. S. LANDRUM, MR. JOHN E. POUND to MISS THURZA L. FLEMING

Died – In this city, on the 14th inst., MR. ENOCH LUNCFORD, aged 74 years.

In Athens, on the 5th inst., MR. GEO. PRINGLE, for several years a resident of that place. All who knew him respected him – he was that noblest specimen of God's handiwork, an honest man.

In Milledgeville, on the 6TH INST, CHARLES H. RICE, Esq. Secretary to the Executive.

In Milledgeville, on the 12th inst, MRS. MARIA COTTON, wife of THOMAS COTTON, in the 45th year of her age. MRS. COTTON was a native of England and has been a resident of this city for about eight years.

Obituary - Departed this life on the 5th inst. in Bibb county, at the residence of his father, ROLIN BIVENS, Esq. JAMES S. BIVENS, in the 22d year of his age. He died of inflammatory rheumatism; his sickness was short and severe, for during the last part of his illness his mind was deranged. He was a young man of promise – had just finished his collegiate course in Oglethorpe University...Some four years ago he joined the Methodist church...

The subject of the following brief notice, ABNER H. FLEWELLEN, M.D. was born in Warren county, Ga. On the 19th May 1800 and died in Wynnton, on the morning of the 28th December, 1849, being 49 years and 7 months of age...

Issue of Jan 29, 1850

Married – In Greenville, Ga. MR. JOHN B. HEARD, to MISS MATTIE HEDEPETH (?), all of that place.

At the residence of J. B. ROWLAND, Esq. Montgomery, Ala, on the 11th inst, by Rev. MR. MORRISON, COL. M.B. MENARD, of Galveston, Texas, to REBCCA (?) MARY, oldest daughter of MRS. SARAH FLUKER, of this city.

In Pulaski county, on the 3d instant, by JOHN A. WYNNE, J.I.C., MR. TURNER POPE, to MISS ABIGAIL MCDUFFIE, all of Pulaski county.

3

In Pulaski county, on the 20th instant, by JOHN A. WYNNE, J.I.C., MR. JOHN A. HANDLET, to MISS CLEOS MIXON, all of Pulaski county.

On the 24th inst, by the Rev. DR. EDWARD W. JONES, JOHN FIELD, Esq., to MISS SARAH E., daughter of DR. DAVID COOPER of Powelton, Hancock county, Ga.

Died — On the 20th inst. at the residence of MR. NATHAN S. TUCKER, in this city, MRS. ELIZABETH MORRIS, aged 71 years. She was born in Nottoway county, Va. in the year 1779, but had resided in Georgia for the last 40 years.

Ten Dollars Reward — Runaway from the subscriber in Jefferson county, on the night of the 20th inst. a negro man named TOM. He is very black, large eyes, and about six feet two inches high; he has also a scar on the left cheek, the result of a blow; he has a remarkably round hand and weighs about 180 lbs. I suppose the boy is endeavoring to get to Sumter co, Ga. as his wife has been taken there lately by MR. G. T. WELLS. The above reward will be given to any person who will deliver him in a safe jail, and any information of said boy thankfully received.

SAMUEL HANNAH

Issue of Feb 12, 1850

Married — In this county, on Tuesday evening, 5th instant, by the Rev. WALTER R. BRANHAM, MR. ALBERT S. (?) ROSS to MISS REBECCA, daughter of THOMAS BAGBY, Esq.

At the same time and place, MR. CHARLES JOHNSON to MISS ELIZA, daughter of THOMAS BAGBY, Esq.

Died — In this city, on Sunday evening last, MR. MICHAEL RILEY, aged 23 years, a native of Savannah, Ga.

In Griffin, on the 5th inst, MISS ROWENA, eldest daughter of NATHAN C. MONROE, Esq. Of Vineville.

In this city, on the 7th inst., MR. H. B. KING.

In Philadelphia, on the 5th inst, Com. DANIEL TURNER, of the U. S. Navy.

Issue of Feb 19, 1850

Married – In Monroe county, on the 12th inst, by the Rev. MR. STEPHENS, Col. JOHN H. JOSSEY, of Griffin, to MISS LUCINDA M. BROWNING, of the former place.

On the 12th inst. At Cornucopia, Ga. By Rev. C. P. BEMAN, A. B. SPRINGS, Esq. Of York, S. C. to MISS JULIA BLANDINS, daughter of JUDGE ELI BAXTER, of the former place.

Died – MRS. THEODOSIDA, wife of THOMAS T. LONG, Esq., and daughter of FRANCIS M. SCARLETT, Esq., of Glynn county, died at their residence near Brunswick on the 11th inst. after a sudden illness of a few days.

Issue of Feb 26, 1850

Married – In Dooly county, on the 19th inst, by the Rev. A. T. HOLMES, JAMES M. JONES of Macon, to MISS A. EMMA BEALLE.

On the 21st inst. By the Rev. W. R. BRANHAM, MR. JOHN T. PRICE to MISS SARAH P. FLANDERS, all of East Macon.

Married – In Bryan county, on the 28th ult. By the Rev. J. S. LAW, MR. E.F. T. ROWLAND of Savannah to MISS MARY WINN, daughter of DR. RAYMOND HARRIS, of the former place.

In Stewart county, on Tuesday evening, the 26th ult. By the Rev. JESSE H. CAMPBELL, MR. SAMUEL Q. BEALL, of Irwinton, Ga. to MISS TABITHA E., daughter of JOHN TALBOT, Esq. Of the former place.

Died – In this city, on the 10th inst, of malignant sore throat, ANN ELIZABETH, infant daughter of DR. J. T. and LOUISA COXE, aged 7 months and 13 days.

On the 25th ult., in Putnam, county, Ga., MR. SETH G. WATSON, formerly of Bibb.

Death of CAPTAIN MAY – The St. Louis Union, of the 19th ult. contains an account of the life and death of this young officer, who won the earliest laurels that were gathered in the late Mexican War. He died, says the Union, in San Francisco, after a short illness from scurvy and bronchitis, produced from New York to that place by the course of Cape Horn. At the period of his death, he was about twenty-seven years of age, and in the very (paper cut off).

Issue of March 19, 1850

PRESTON W. FARRAR (?) Esq. Speaker of the House of Representatives of the State of Louisiana, died at Baton Rouge, on Thursday last, after a brief illness. His loss is deeply regretted by all who had the pleasure of his acquaintance.

Death of a brother of HENRY CLAY – The last surviving full brother of the Hon. HENRY CLAY, the Rev. PORTER

CLAY, died at the city of Camden, in Arkansas, on the 16th ultimo, in the 71st year of his age. It is said that, like his distinguished brother, he was, in all the attainments of education, self-made. (unreadable)

Married – In this city, on the 16th (?) inst, by Rev. E. H. MYERS, DR. W. W. HOLMES of Fairfield District, S. C. to MISS SUSAN E. ELLISON, of this place.

Near Cassville, on the 6th (?) inst, by Rev. C. W. HOWARD, MR. HENRY A. TARVER of Baker county, to MISS ELIZABETH G. daughter of Col. Wm. Solomon (?) of Cass county.

Died – In this city, on the morning of the 12th (?) inst. In the 62d year of his age, MR. EDMUND BLAKE. MR. BLAKE was a native of Orange county, North Carolina, but for many years a highly respectable merchant of Fayettsville. In 1839, he removed to this city, where he resided until his death. He leaves a large circle of relatives and friends to mourn his death.

Issue of April 2, 1850

Death of JOHN C. CALHOUN – long article

Issue of April 16, 1850

Married – At Longstreet in Pulaski county on the 26th ult. By the Rev. JOHN CAMPBELL, MR. GEORGE W. JORDAN, Esq. Of Hawkinsville to MISS ANN REBECCA youngest daughter of MR. GEORGE WALLER.

Issue of April 23, 1850

Died – In this city, of Consumption, on the 10th inst. in the 40th year of his age, DR. W. E. FULWOOD, Assistant Surgeon in the U. S. army. DR. FULWOOD was born in

Clark county in this State – an after preparing himself for college, entered Franklin University, where he graduated in 1829. After completing his collegiate course at the University of his native state he commenced the study of medicine. In 1831 he commenced its practice. His success as a practitioner was such as to command the respect and confidence of all who knew him. In 1839 he joined the Army where he remained in the active discharge of the duties of his profession, until a few months preceding his death. He was attached to General TAYLOR'S Medical Staff at Corpus Christi, where he continued until the command of that officer was withdrawn from Mexico. He was present at the battles of Resaca, Palo Alto, Monterey and Buena Vista, and underwent all the hardships and fatigues of that memorable campaign. His exposure during the war, seriously impaired his health, and planted in his system the seeds of the disease which terminated his life. He leaves a wide circle of relatives and friends to mourn his death. His remains were interred at Rose Hill Cemetery near this city on Thursday last with appropriate honors by the Volunteer Corps of the city.

On the 14th inst. At the house of MR. JOSEPH B. ANDREWS in this county, MR. SOLOMON GROCE, aged 28 years. He was one of the noble band of patriots who volunteered to fight in the battles of his country in the Mexican War.

In Macon county on the 11th inst. MR. JAMES BASSETT, in the 35th year of his age. MR. B. connected himself with the Baptist Church in 1835...

Issue of April 30, 1850

Melancholy Accident – Col. C. G. DERUSSY and his three sons, all of age, were drowned in Sibley's Lake, in the neighborhood of Notchitochen, a few days since. They had gone out in a small boat, fishing, and were caught in a squall – the boat upset and they were drowned. A gentleman by the name of PALMER who was with them, swam to the shore. The bodies have not been recovered. Col. DERUSSY was educated at West Point and for many years was in the army. He was colonel of the Louisiana Regiment in the Mexican War, and had command at Tampico.

Married – In this city, by the Rev. MR. HOOKER, Col. A. H. DOUGLASS of Summerville, Tenn. to MISS ELIZA B, daughter of the late DR. R. H. RANDOLPH.

Died – Recently at his residence in Oawichee, Ala, Maj. DAVID C. ROSE, formerly of Meriwether county, Ga...His remains were carried to Greenville, Ga. whither those of his son had so recently preceded them and were interred with the usual rites and ceremonies of Free Masonry. Columbus Times

Issue of May 7, 1850

Married – On the 2d inst. by the Rev. SYLVANUS LANDRUM, Col. WM F. WILBURN at Penfield, to MISS FRANCES I. WILLET, of East Macon.

In Forsyth, on the 2d inst, by the Rev. MR. OVERBY, CINCINNATUS PEOPLES, Esq. of Athens, to MISS ELIZA_____, daughter of E. C. CABANISS (?), Esq.

Died – In this city, on the 26th ult. of Tubercular Consumption, MRS. LOUISA E. COXE, consort of DR. J. T. COXE of Forsyth, aged twenty-five years 2_ days.

Issue of May 14, 1850

Married – On the 25th ult., at the residence of Gen. W. BAILEY in Jefferson county, by the Rev. P. P. SMITH,

DOCTOR THOMPSON B. LAMAR, of Oxford, Georgia, to MISS SARAH B, daughter of Gen. WM BAILEY, of Jefferson county, Florida.

Issue of May 21, 1850

Married – In Vineville, yesterday morning by the Rev. DR. ELLISON, MR. GEORGE M. LOGAN to MISS PAULINE, daughter of THOMAS HARDEMAN, Esq.

In Columbus, on the 8th (?) inst, by the Rev. WM. M. CRUMLEY, Col HENRY J. LAMAR, of Macon, to MISS VALERIA B, eldest daughter of WILEY E. JONES, Esq, of Columbus.

Died – In this city, on the 18th (?) inst, in the 77th year of his age, MR. ROBERT CUNNINGHAM. MR. CUNNINGHAM, was a native of South Carolina, but for the last half century resided in this state.

Death of a Clergyman – It is with no common feelings, says the Columbus Enquirer, of the 14th inst, that we are called upon to announce the death of Rev. W. D. CAIRUS (?), late Pastor of the Trinity Church of this city.

Issue of May 28, 1850

Extraordinary case of Longevity – DINAH, an old negress, died in Norfolk, Va. a few days ago at the age of one hundred and twenty three years! She was a servant in a family residing at the Great Bridge, when the memorable battle was fought there in 1775, between Col WOODFORD'S Virginia troops and the British grenadiers, under Captain FORDYCE, and was at that time, a grandmother – a fact which attests her age. She was blind for a number of years, but recovered her sight when past her hundredth year, so that she could see to thread a needle, and having lost all her teeth, she cut an entire new

10

set about the same time. She was remarkably sprightly and industrious to the last. Norfolk Herald

Issue of June 4, 1850

Married – In this city, on the 21st ult. by Rev. MR. BRANHAM, MR. ISAAC COMINGOS, of Griffin to MISS SARAH CAROLINE TISDALE of Griffin, of this city.

In Washington county, on the 27th ult. by the Hon HERSCHEL V. JOHNSON, Col. JAMES S. HOOK, of Sandersville, to MISS EMILY J., daughter of Maj. DANIEL HARRIS of Washington county.

Died – At his residence in Talbot county, on the 24thult, after a confinement of some six weeks, GEORGE R. MCCANTS, in the 44th year of his age. The deceased was esteemed and beloved by all who knew him; he has left a wife and three children besides a large circle of friends and acquaintances to mourn his death.

$15 Reward – Runaway from the subscriber, on or about the 10th of April, my negro boy by the name of JACOB or JAKE. Said boy is about 27 or 28 years old, about six feet one inch high, weighs about 170 or 175 pounds, very dark complected, has a very high forehead, and when spoken to speaks slow, and throws his head back and stands erect, but when walking leans forward, has very large eyes, large mouth, with a good set of teeth. He is very accommodating, and quick in obliging any one when requested. In walking he throws his toes out. I will give the above reward for him, if lodged in any safe jail so that I can get him, or $25 delivered to me in Milledgeville.

A. C. DEVEREUX

11

Brought to Jail, in Macon, Bibb county, on the 25th May, a negro boy who calls his name BEN, about 19 or 20 years old, dark complexion, front teeth out, about 5 feet 6 or 7 inches high, and says he belongs to NORRIL JONES of Meriwether county, Ga. The owner is requested to come forward, prove property, pay charges and take him away, or he will be dealt with as the law directs.

WILLIS H. HUGHES,
Jailor

Brought to Jail in Macon, Bibb county, on the 28th May, a negro boy who calls his name DANIEL KING, about 40 years old, dark complexion, about 5 feet 1 or 2 inches high, thin visage, and spare made, and says he belongs to one MR. SHARP, a negro trader and left him near this place. The owner is requested to come forward, prove property, pay charges and take him away, or he will be dealt with as the law directs.

WILLIS H. HUGHES,
Jailor

Brought to jail in Macon, Bibb county, on the 29th of May, a negro boy who says his name is GEORGE, about 17 or 18 years old, about five feet five or six inches high and blind in one eye, rather light complexion, and says he belongs to JAMES FLEMING of Monroe county. The owner is requested to come forward, prove property, pay charges, and take him away, or he will be dealt with as the law directs.

WILLIS H. HUGHES,
Jailor

12

Married – On Monday morning 10th inst, MR. E. S. ROGERS to MISS CATHERINE MCG_____, both of this city.

Died – In this city, on the 15th (?) ult., of scarlet fever, SARAH LUCINDA, infant daughter of E. O. AND C_____M. WHITEHEAD, aged 9 months and 4 days.

Died – In this city on Saturday morning last, 8th June 1850, in the 69th (?) year of his age SCOTT CRAY, Esq. a native of Onslow (?) county, North Carolina but for the last forty years a citizen of Georgia and for twenty-four years____a resident of this city. The Raleigh, Fayetteville, Wilmington and Newburg papers will please copy.

Issue of June 18, 1850

Died – April 8 (?), 1850, at sea, DOCTOR JOHN S. WHITTLE, Passed Assistant Surgeon in the United States Navy. (Long article, difficult to read)

Issue of June 25, 1850

Brought to Jail – In Jacksonville, Telfair county, on the 17th day of May, a negro boy who calls his name JEFFREY, and says he belongs to HENRY BASEMORE (?) of Houston county and that he has been runaway about twelve months. He is about 36 years old, stout built, and dark complexion and is about 5 feet 11 inches high.

W. S. MOORE, Act'g
Jailor

Married – On the 16th inst, by the Rev. H. C. ____NEDY, MR. P. V. WILSON, to MISS ELIZABETH ASHLEY, all of Pulaski county.

Married – On the 25th June, by the Rev. J. P. DUNCAN, MR. JOSEPH R. BANKS of Pike county to MISS AMANDA M. youngest daughter of ARCHIBALD DAVIS, Esq. of Monroe county.

Died – In Vineville, on the 24th ult. MISS MARY ANN JAFFIE, aged about 46 years.

In Dahlonega, Ga., on the 21st ult. at 6 o'clock, P. M. MRS. SUSAN R. wife of Col. A. W. REDDING, Superintendent U. S. Branch Mint, and daughter of the late DRURY JACKSON...MRS. R. lived 42 years lacking one day, thirty of which were spent in communion with the M. E. Church.

Brought to Jail in Hawkinsville, Pulaski county, on the 10th June, a negro boy who says his name is PETER, and that he belongs to WESLEY MAYFIELD of Scriven county, Ga. and was stolen from his plantation some four or five weeks since. Said boy is about 18 or 19 years old, dark complexion, 5 feet 6 or 8 inches high...

DANIEL GRIFFIN, Jailor

$25 Reward – Runaway from the subscriber on the 25th of last month, a negro man named CHARLES, 23 or 4 years old, he is a dark mulatto, about 6 feet high, weighs about 180 lbs. Wears whiskers, has rather small eyes, has some worts on his left hand and has cut a wort off his middle finger of the left hand lately, and parred off the end of the finger half way the nail. CHARLES was raised in Cass county by Major JOHN DAWSON, he can write and no doubt he will travel under a pass or free papers of his own writing, he is well acquainted in the Cherokee county, and in Tennessee and Augusta, Ga., Charleston, S. C., and Savannah, Ga; he is very likely and very smart, can tell a lie with as much assurance as any negro, he talks with

14

great firmness. I have no doubt but that he will attempt to get to Ohio or some other free state, he may pass under the name of CHARLES BLAKE or CHARLES SMITH or some other fictitious name. I will pay the above reward for his delivery to me in Macon, or $20 for his arrest and confinement in any safe jail so that I can get him.

SPENCER RILEY

Issue of July 9, 1850

Brought to Jail in Macon, Bibb county, a negro boy named JOHNSON, about 16 or 17 years of age, light complexion, about 5 feet 6 inches high and says he belongs to JOSEPH SANFORD of Jasper county.

W. H. HUGHES, Jailor

Married – In Milledgeville, on the 21st ult. by Rev. DR. TALMAGE, JOHN JONES, Esq. of Carroll, to MISS SUSAN C., oldest daughter of PETER J. WILLIAMS.

In Muscogee county, on the 20th ult, at the residence of WM R (?) ROCKMORE, by R. W. CARNES (?) Esq, MR. THOMAS HULT of Jones county, to MISS MARY RENFRON.

Died – In Bibb county, on the 3d inst, MR. JEDEDIAH WILLET, aged 82 (?) years, formerly of Norwich, Connecticut, but for the last nineteen or twenty years a citizen of this State.

On the 18(?) ult. at the residence of her father, Capt. DANIEL BIRD, near Monticello, Florida, MISS SARAH OLIVER BIRD, in the 20th year of her age.

In Milledgeville, on the 9th inst, MRS. ELIZA M. JARRATT, wife of DR. W. A. JARRATT, aged 24 years.

15

At his residence in Talbot county, Georgia, on the 30th of June, Col. JOSEPH RILEY, in the seventy-first year of his age.

The subject of the above notice was born in Orange county, North Carolina, January 7th, 1780, and emigrated to Georgia with his father in 1796, and settled in Green county...In 1859, he moved to Talbot county, and settled the place on which he died. (long article)

Issue of July 23, 1850

Died – Of scarlet fever, on the 10th inst, in Crawford county, JULIUS KINSEY, eldest son of JOHN M. and MARGARET A. HAVLES (?) aged 4 years 6 months and 10 days.

Issue of August 6, 1850

Married – On the 28th July, by the Rev. JOHN H. CALDWELL, MR. ABNER F. REDDING, of Macon to MISS ANN ELIZA, daughter of MR. ALEXANDER SMITH of Houston county.

In Athens, on Wednesday morning, 31st ult., by Rev. E. W. SPIER, DR. O. A. LOCHRANE, of Savannah to MISS VICTORIA FRANCES, daughter of Col. H.G. LAMAR of Athens.

Died – In this city, on the 29th ult. MRS. ELIZA B. HOLZENDORF, aged about 41 years – wife of MR. JOHN HOLZENDORF.

Issue of August 13, 1850

Died – In this city, on the 5th inst, GEORGE B, youngest son of MARTHA D. and HARDY MORRIS, aged 11 months and 8 days.

16

In this city, on the 8th inst, MRS. PHEBE, wife of SAMUEL ATKINSON, of this city...

On the 1st inst, at the residence of his parents, in Thomas county, RICHARD, son of DR. THOMAS B. and ELIZABETH WINN, aged eight years and a few days.

Issue of August 20, 1850

Died – In this city, ANN ELIZA, daughter of RICHARD B. and ELIZA LYNN, aged 18 months. Funeral will take place, from their residence, this day, at 9 o'clock a.m.

In Cartersville, on the 9th inst, after an illness of about 10 hours, of Bilious Cholic, MR. COLEMAN PITTS, aged about 50 years. The deceased was a highly respectable citizen of Cass county, and has left a large family and many friends to mourn his sudden death.

Issue of August 27, 1850

Runaway – From the subscriber on the 21st inst a negro man named STEPNEY, about 24years old, he is of black complexion, about 6 feet 5 or 6 inches high, weighs about 195 lbs, has a scar under one of his eyes, and some lumps on his breast supposed to be bruised by the whip, has the appearance of a limp when he walks. Said boy is very stout built, and is very intelligent – I will pay a reward of ten dollars for his apprehension and confinement in any safe Jail in this State so that I can get him.

R. R. MINSHEW

Issue of September 3, 1850

Married – On the 22d ult. by the Rev. JOHN W. TALLY, MR. WM. T. HOLDERNESS of Leon county, Fla. To MISS S. J. SCOTT of Troup county, Ga.

Runaway – From the subscriber, near Montpelier, Monroe county, on the 26th ult. a negro boy by the name of LEROY, about 20 years old, and about 5 feet 5 in high, square built, dark copper color and roman nose, he took with him a good fur hat and cloth cap, 2 round coats, three pair pants, one striped vest, one common blue sack, one striped dress coat, one pair shoes, one pair fine boots, and his violin, on which he performs. LEROY was born and raised in Yorkville District, S. C. and was owned by HENRY H. DRENON and it is likely he may try to make his way back. Any person who will deliver said boy to me, or confine him so that I can get him, shall be liberally rewarded.

JOHN MCCOLLUM
Russelville, P.O. Monroe
Co., Ga.

Issue of September 10, 1850

Distressing death from Hydrophobia – We learn from the Natchez Free Trader, that MISS SARAH FULTON, a lovely and interesting young lady of nineteen years, belonging to Franklin county, Miss. Came to her death on Sunday, the 4th inst, from the bite of a mad dog about four weeks previous. The Free Trader says: MISS FULTON, on Saturday morning, felt shooting pains from the place where she had been bitten in the arm, ascending towards her neck and throat, but was well enough to ride some distance to attend a Temperance barbecue. The day being hot, much water was drunk; and while attempting to drink, the poor girl felt an unaccountable spasm or chill, pervade her frame, which prevented her from drinking. As she rode home she grew worse, and told the gentleman who accompanied her that she would die of canine madness. The paroxyms soon became dreadful; her mouth constantly filling with saliva, and throwing out foam, which had to be wiped away constantly. Her distressed and hoarse

18

breathing could be heard for many hundred yards. Nature sank under the awful struggle in about twenty-four hours, and death came to her relief on Sunday evening, the day after she was taken ill. What is most awful, and fills the community far and near with a pervading gloom, is the fact that MRS. FULTON, a widow and the mother of MISS SARAH, was bitten much worse than her daughter, by the same dog; a negro, belonging to them, was also bitten; neither of whom, as yet has felt the symptoms of the disease.

Died – In Hawkinsville, on the 1st inst, RILEY WHITFIELD, infant son of S. M. and HARRIET MANNING aged about three years.

$ Reward – Will be paid for information of the whereabouts of one M. J. WILLIAMSON – a carriage trimmer by trade. He left the city on the 19th of August. In order to baffle pursuit, I understand he has since reported himself as dead. I will pay the above reward to any one who will satisfy me that his last words are true. It is supposed that he went from this place to Athens. All honest men should be on their guard against this unmitigated scoundrel.

Issue of September 17, 1850

Brought to Jail in Bibb county, about the 20th of August, a negro boy by the name of JIM, who says he belongs to a MR. SIMMONS, a negro trader. Said boy is 16 or 17 years of age, stout and likely, and says he was lately purchased in Virginia. The owner of said negro is requested to come forward, prove property, pay charges and take him away.

WILLIS H. HUGHES, Jailor

The Rev. BISHOP BASCOM died at Louisville, Kentucky, on 7th inst.

Washington Lodge, No. 46 – The recent demise of Brother JAMES BELAND. (long article)

Married – In East Macon, on the 12th inst, by Rev. WALTER H. BRANHAM, MR. WILLIAM F. SIMS to MISS CATHARINE M. SULLIVAN, both of this city.

Died – In this city, on Saturday last the 14th instant, MRS. SARAH ISRAELINE STROBEL, consort of the Rev. P. A. STROBEL, and youngest daughter of the late ISRAEL FLEET, of Effingham county, Ga.

Issue of September 24, 1850

$20 Reward – Ranaway from the subscriber's plantation, on the Ocmulgee, near Houses Creek, Irwin county, my two negro fellows WILL and JIM; WILL is 23 years of age, 5 feet 7 or 8 inches high, of dark complexion; can be identified by a scar on the back of one of his hands, inflicted by an axe, between the thumb and the index finger. Also, a small knot or lump on the back of his neck, caused by a____. JIM is 17 years of age, 5 feet 5 or 6 inches high, of yellow complexion, with a down look. They will not be apt to separate, having been raised together; they are both intelligent and plausible. It is possible that they have made their way to the up country, under the auspices of an abductor. The above reward will be paid for the two, or $10 for either delivered at my plantation, or any safe jail in the State, so that I can get them.

JAMES HOLLINGSWORTH

Married – In this city, on Thursday evening last, by the Hon KEELIN COOK, E. F., to MISS MATILDA ROBERTS, of this city.

20

On the 15th inst, by the Rev. W. F. SMITH, MR. W. E. JAMES, of Monroe county, to MISS FRANCES A. MORAN, of Crawford county, Ga.

Died – In Twiggs county, on the 3d inst, MRS. NANCY SMITH, consort of Capt. BENJAMIN B. SMITH, in the 57th year of her age. The subject of this notice was, for 12 years previous to her death, a devoted member of the Baptist Church...

Issue of October 1, 1850

$50 Reward – Runaway from the subscriber on Sunday night last, a negro woman named MARY, about 24 years old, 5 feet 3 or 4 inches high, dark complected, has a mark between her eye and nose, kidney feet, and has remarkable large legs and arms. The undersigned has strong reasons to believe, that said woman has been enticed and carried away by a white man. The above reward will be paid for proof to convict any person for enticing away or harboring said negro, or a reward of ten dollars will be paid for her delivery to me, or lodged in any jail, where I can get her.

J.R. MCELMURRAY

Died – On the 19th ult., by a fall from a building at his mills, MR. JOSEPH WILLET of East Macon. MR. WILLET was born in Norwich, Connecticut and removed to Georgia in his eighteenth year. He died in his 53d year – had resided for the last 35 years in Macon, and was, it is believed, the very first inhabitant of the city – felled the first tree...

On Sunday the 22d ult., at his residence in Upson county, Georgia, BURWELL HOWELL, in the sixty-first year of his age. He was a member of the Methodist Episcopal church and class leader for a number of years previous to his death...

Issue of October 8, 1850

Married – In this city, on the 6th inst, by Judge COOK, MR. WM. SIMS to MISS GEORGIANNA ARNOLD, all of this city.

In Matagorda, Texas, on the 13th June last, Col. HENRY LAURENCE KINNEY, of Corpus Christi, to MRS. MARY BELLFIELD HERBERT.

Obiturary – Departed this life, on the morning of the 30th ult. at her residence in Bibb county, MRS. AMY G. consort of EDMUND GILBERT, in the sixty-seventh year of her age. She has left an affectionate husband and a numerous offspring…

Issue of October 15, 1850

Married – On the 8th inst by Rev. W. C. CLEVELAND, MR. JOHN B. FOWLER to MISS SUSAN HAMMOCK, all of Crawford county.

Runaway – from the subscriber living in Jasper county, a negro boy by the name of LEWIS, rather copper colored, spare made, five feet 6 or 7 inches high, and about 23 years of age. LEWIS is sprightly and intelligent. I will give a reward of $20 for the delivery of said boy tome or fifteen dollars for his confinement in any Jail in the state.

MARCUS L. SMITH

Died – In Titus (?) county, Texas on the 25th Aug. DANIEL L. WALL, in the 35th year of his age. (rest of article is difficult to read).

<u>Issue of Oct 22, 1850</u>

Married – On Lookout Mountain, near Chattanooga, Tenn., on the 18th instant, by the Hon. AUGUSTUS R. WRIGHT, JOHN C. BURCH, Esq. of Spring Place, Ga. and MISS LICIE NEWELL, of the former place.

Died – In Chattanooga, on the 4th inst, JOSEPH THOMAS, son of J.A.R. and MARY A. BENNETT, aged 10 months and 2 days.

In this county, on the 13th inst, MR. ABRAM MASSEY, aged about 60 years – a native of North Carolina, but for about 20 years, of Jones co., Ga.

<u>Issue of October 29, 1850</u>

Married – In Dalton, on the 10th inst, by the Rev. LEVI BROTHERTON, THOS T. CHRISTIAN, Editor of the Dalton Times and MISS CAROLINE M. ROBERTS.

Died – At his residence in Wynnton, near Columbus, Ga., on the 11th inst MR. CASAM EMER BARTLETT, in the 57th year of his age, a native of New Hampshire, but long a resident of this state.

<u>Issue of November 6, 1850</u>

Death of a Member of Congress – The Hon. JOHN L. HARMANSON, Representative of the Third Congressional District of Louisiana died at his residence in Point Coupee Parish on the 25th ult.

Obituary – Departed this life, on Wednesday, 23d ult. In the sixty-sixth year of his age, MARK D. CLARKE, Esq., a native of Savannah, but for many years a citizen of Bibb county.

Died – In this city, on the 29 ult., ANN MARIA, only daughter of JOHN K. and ELIZABETH HARMAN, aged years, 6 months and 12 days.

At the residence of his son in this city, MR. THOMAS SPRINGER, aged about 90 years. MR. S. was born in Union District, S. C., but had long been a citizen of this state. He had for a large part of his life been an humble and consistent member of the Baptist Church. His end was peaceful.

In the city of Savannah, on the 31st ult. MISS GEORGIA ANN STARR YOKUM, aged 16 years and 6 months, eldest daughter of JAMES YOKUM of Savannah. MISS Y. bore with patience and resignation her painful bed of sickness, having had the inflammatory fever for thirty- two days without intermission. She became a member of the Methodist Episcopal Church, a few months before her decease. She has left numerous relatives and friends to mourn her loss. She died in peace.

Issue of November 12, 1850

Married – In this city, on Tuesday evening last, by Rev. JOHN C. HOOKER, MR. A. B. ADAMS to MISS HENRIETTA HOLLINGSWORTH.

On Wednesday morning, 6th inst. by the Rev. J. F. POSTELL, MR. HENRY E. MOORE, of this city, to MISS GEORGIA A. RODGERS, daughter of JOHN C. RODGERS of Macon county.

$10 Reward – Will be paid for the apprehension of my negro woman CAROLINE. She is about 20 years old, about 5 feet 3 or 4 inches high, rather bright complexion but not a mulatto, a full head of hair generally, well combed and very likely. I have reason to believe she is lurking about Macon, or in the vicinity.

CYNTHIA TAYLOR

Issue of November 19, 1850

Obituary – Died Shasta city, Upper California, 6th of September, after a severe and painful illness, CHARLES HENRY HULL, MD, a native of Burlington, Vt., aged thirty years.

Issue of November 26, 1850

Married – In Monroe county, on Wednesday evening, 20th inst, by the Rev. MR. DUNCAN, MR. JAMES Y. MIMS of Houston county, to MISS SARAH JOHNSON, of Monroe county, Ga.

Issue of December 3, 1850

Death of General DANIEL NEWMAN - ...he died at his residence in Walker county, Georgia, on Monday last...(difficult to read)

Married – In this city, on the 28th ult., by the Rev. R. HOOKER, MR. T. R. BLOOM, to MISS ANNA E. FLUKER.

In East Macon, on the 26th ult. by the Rev. S. LANDRUM, MR. NATHANIEL COATES to MISS SUSAN V. ADAMS.

On the 5th ult., in Christ church, St. Louis, by Rev. DR. HAWKS, Hon. EDWARD CARRINGTON CABELL of

Florida, to MISS ANN MARIA WILCOX, daughter of MRS. GEN. ASHLEY.

At Wilmington, N. C. on the 18th ult., by Rev. DR. DRANE, GEN WADDY THOMPSON, late Minister Plenipotentiary to Mexico, to MISS CORNELIA A. JONES, daughter of Col. JOHN W. JONES, of the former place.

Two hundred and thirty dollars reward – I will pay two hundred dollars for the apprehension and delivery to me of my boy PRINCE, he ranaway from the Southwestern Railroad, Houston county, in November 1849, went from there to Talbot, thence to Marion county, where he was when last heard from. PRINCE is about 24 years old, brown color, straight and well made, weighs about 165 lbs, 5 feet 10 inches high. I will also pay ten dollars each for the apprehension of NED, a tall black man, bad teeth in front, about 30 years old. PATRICK, a small man, brown color, very rough face, about 25 years old, and DIMON, a short heavy built black man, 35 or 40 years old. The last three Negroes were bought in Charleston and are no doubt trying to get back.

JAMES DEAN

Issue of December 10, 1850

Married – In Sparta, Hancock county, by the Rev. RICHARD LANE, MR. LAVOISIEUR L. LAMAR of Macon, to MISS LOUISA E. HARRIS of Hancock county.

In Eatonton, on the 24th ult., by Rev. W. P. ARNOLD, Gen. WM. F. BRANTLEY of Savannah, to MISS FANNIR ADAMS, of the former place.

Died – In Culloden, on the 30th ul.t, of Typhoid Pneumonia, MISS A. H. HODGES, in the fifteenth year of her age.

26

Issue of December 24, 1850

Married – On Tuesday evening, 17th inst, by K. J. T. LITTLE, Esq., MR. ALFRED PRATT, to MISS SARAH M. ALLISON, all of Harris county.

Obituary – Departed this life, at his residence in Baker county, on the 15th instant, MR. JAMES C. BARTLETT, in the 35th year of his age. He left a wife, three children and numerous friends to mourn his early death.

Issue of January 7, 1851

Death of Editor – The Wilmington papers of last week, announce the death, in that city, on the 30th ult., of HENRY J. TOOLE, Esq., editor of the Aurora of that place.

Death of Rev. EDWARD NEUFVILLE – The Savannah Republican of Tuesday last, announces the death on the 1st, of the Rev. EDWARD NEUFVILLE, D. D. – aged forty-eight years, on the Christmas day just passed. The deceased was a native of the city of Washington, and was first installed as Rector of the Episcopal Church in Prince William's Parish, S. C. from which place he was called to the Rectorship of Christ church, Savannah. During a period of twenty-three years, he performed the pastoral duties of that church, having seen, in this time, nearly all the other churches of the Diocese of Georgia grow up around him.

Married – In Columbus on the 18th ult., by the Rev. MR. TICKNOR, MR. WM. P. AUBREY, of Mobile, to MISS ROSA M., fifth daughter of the late Hon. JOHN FORSYTH.

Died – On Friday evening the 27th of December, at his lat residence in Dooly county, JOHN MATTHEWS, aged ninety four years. He served as a Soldier in the

Revolutionary War, and then settled in North Carolina, from whence he came to Georgia. He died respected by all as an honest man.

Forty Dollars Reward – Ranaway from the subscriber during Christmas with my two boys BOB and TOM. BOB is about 32 years old, 5 feet 5 inches high, well built, slightly grey headed, weighing about 155 lbs; speaks the low county brogue; black color; wore off dark striped pants, black frock coat with pockets on each side, black satin vest and black cloth cap. He sometimes calls himself GREEN. TOM is 21 years old, about 5 feet 6 inches high, well built, not so dark as BOB; weighs about 160 lbs, has a small scar on the side of the nose next to the left eye; wore off brown mixed satinet pants with a rent sewed up on the left knee; dark tweed coat and black cloth cap. I will give $20 apiece for their delivery to me and pay all necessary expenses that may be incurred by whoever arrests them. They are lurking in the city somewhere, or about the plantations around or may be making their way to Savannah, Charleston, Marietta or Augusta.

JAMES A. KNIGHT

Issue of January 14, 1851

Robbery of the Mail – An agent of the Post Office arrested MR. H. B. KIMBROUGH, of Columbus, in this city, some ten days since, charged with robbing the mail of $6,000, which was mailed at Cheraw, S. C., on the 29th of November last. MR. K. confessed the crime, and gave up $5,320 of the money. He had been engaged temporarily as a clerk in the Post Office at Columbus, where he committed the theft. KIMBROUGH, in default of bail, has been committed to Jail to await his trial at the next term of the United States Circuit Court for the District of Georgia.

Married – In Irwinton, Ga. on the 8th inst. at the residence of MR. LEWIS GARDNER, by SAMUEL BEALL, Esq., MR. ALEXANDER BAUM, to MISS AMELIA FRIEDLOTH, formerly of Prussia.

Issue of January 21, 1851

Married – In Crawford county, on 16th inst, by the Rev. W. C. CLEVELAND, ROBERT C. PARHAM, to MISS MARY JANE HAMMACK.

Died – At the residence of his mother, MRS. ELVIRA FLEWELLEN, in Wynnton, near this city, on Saturday morning, the 4th inst, ALEXANDER HOLOWAY FLEWELLEN, aged seven years, seven months and six days. ALEXANDER was the youngest child and only son of his mother...

Issue of January 28, 1851

Married – On the 2d inst, by Rev. N. M. CRAWFORD, Prof. JOS. E. WILLET, of Mercer University, to MISS EMILY A. H. daughter of Rev. B. M. SANDERS of Penfield.

Died – At his residence in Putnam county, on the 7th day of this month, PETTON HOLT, Esq., in the 77th year of his age.

Issue of February 4, 1851

Married – On the 21st ult., by the Rev. JA

MES WILLIAMSON, MR. J. A. MERIWETHER to MRS. A. E. WEEKS, both of Hawkinsville.

Died – On the 19th ult., near Tallahassee, Fla., MRS. ELIZA BRANCH, wife of the Hon. JOHN BRANCH, formerly of Halifax county, N. C.

Issue of February 11, 1851

Horrible – About 1 o'clock on Friday night, a small frame dwelling in Vineville, occupied as a residence by MRS. SWINDON, was discovered to be on fire. Upon discovering the flames, the neighbors repaired to the building, but found the doors and windows barred so that it was impossible to enter or stop the progress of the flames. The water bucket was also removed from the well-rope so that no water could be procured on the premises. From these and other circumstances, it is supposed that the wretched woman, in a fit of insanity, murdered her four children, and then set fire to the house, in which all were consumed. A Coroner's Jury was held on the case the next day, but we have not been favored with its verdict.

Fatal Rencounter – A rencounter took place in East Macon, on Saturday night, between WILLIAM EDWARDS and _____WEST, which resulted in the death of the latter. EDWARDS had just been pardoned from the Penitentiary, where he had been confined for an assault with intent to murder. He has made his escape.

Death of MR. AUDUBON, the Distinguished Ornithoogist.

Death of Major BUTLER – Major PIERCE BUTLER, brother of Col. WM. O. BUTLER, late candidate for the office of Vice President of the United States, a distinguished lawyer, and for many years a member of the Legislature of Kentucky, died on the 15th inst, at Louisville.

DAVID S. KAUFFMAN, a member of the House of Representatives from Texas, died on the 31st ult. Disease – affection of the heart.

MRS. MARTHA MYERS, the last survivor of the massacre of Wyoming, died at Kingston, Luzerne county, on the 4th of January, aged 89. Her father, THOMAS BENNET, was one of the forty white men who built the stockade called "Forty Fort".

DR. MCWHIR – This aged and venerable man whose name is familiar to most of our readers, died, we regret to state, on the 31st ult. An Irishman by birth, DR. MCWHIR emigrated to this country about the year 1783, settled soon after at Alexandria, Va., where he taught school for several years, and thence removed to Georgia, with a view to take charge of Richmond county Academy, but finally settled at Sunbury, at which place and its vicinity he continued successfully the profession of a teacher... He died at MR. ROSEWELL KING'S in Liberty county, in his ninety-second year. Savannah Republican

Married - In the city of Macon, at the residence of, and by the Rev. JOHN M. FIELD, on Thursday evening, the 30th January ult., HENRY G. ROSS, Esq, Clerk of the Superior Court of Bibb county, to MISS AMELIA T. ROSS.

In Jones county, on the 4th inst. by the Rev. C. R. JEWETT, MR. THOMAS H. MORRIS, to MISS HARRIET M. eldest daughter of Maj. LEROY SINGLETON, both of Jones county, Ga.

In this city on the 6th inst, by the Rev. MR. HOOKER, MR. E. L. TILLINGHAST, to MISS LUCRETIA CUNNINGHAM, both of this city.

31

In New Orleans, on the 26th ult., by the Rev. MR. NEVILLE, Gen. MIRABEAU B. LAMAR to MISS HENRIETTA M. MAFFIT, both of Texas.

Died – In this city, on the 3d inst, MRS. ELIZA W. LAMAR, wife of DR. THOMAS R. LAMAR.

In this city, on the 8th inst, MRS. CARVER, wife of ROBERT CARVER, Esq. and daughter of Major J. H. HARDAWAY, of this city.

Horrible Affair – The New Orleans Picayune says: A gentleman recently from Holmes county, Miss., has detailed to us the particulars of a dreadful scene, which occurred a few days since near Lexington in that county. An engagement had existed for some time between a MR. TATE and MISS SHEPPERD, in the Harlen Creek district, in that county, to which however, the father of the young lady refused consent. The young couple had agreed to run away for the purpose of getting married, and for that purpose were to start from a wedding party held in the neighborhood. We have not heard what intervened to excite the young man's passions. He met the young lady as arranged, at the party, and asked her publicly whether she was ready to fulfill her promise and go with him, and on her declining, he drew a pistol, shot her dead in the room, and attempted to destroy himself, but in this was frustrated, and is now in Lexington Jail on the charge of murder.

Issue of February 18, 1851

Death of HERR REYNINGER, the Wirewalker.

Married – In this city, on Thursday evening last, by the Rev. DR. ELLISON, M. M. MASON, Esq. of Vineville, to MISS E. J. ROBINSON, of Macon.

Danger of Kissing a Woman Against Her Will – A curious case was recently tried at the Middlesex Sessions, England. THOMAS SAVERLAUD, the prosecutor, stated that he was in the tap room where the defendant, CAROLINE NEWTON, and her sister, who had come from Birmingham, were present. The latter jokingly observed that she had promised her sweetheart that no man should kiss her while absent. It being holyday time, SAVERLAUD considered this a challenge and caught hold of her and kissed her. The young woman took it as a joke, but her sister, the defendant, said she would like a little of that fun as he pleased. He then tried to do it, and they fell to the ground. On rising, the woman struck him. He again tried to kiss her, and in the scuffle, she bit off his nose, which she spit out of her mouth. The action was brought to recover damages for the loss of the nose. The defendant said he had no business to kiss her; if she wanted kissing, she had a husband to kiss her, a better looking man than the prosecutor was. The jury without hesitation, acquitted her, and the chairman said, "that if any man attempted to kiss a woman against her will, she had a right to bite off his nose if she had a fancy for doing it."

Issue of February 25, 1851

Death of Maj. DAVEMAC – This gentleman died in New York, after an illness of thirty-six hours. He was the friend and confidant of Gen. JACKSON, and served with great distinction under that brave chieftain...

Death of General BEM (difficult to read)

Married – On the morning of the 17th inst, by the Rev. MR. SHANKLIN, MR. GEORGE B. CARHART, of New York, to MISS MARY E. ROSE, eldest daughter of MR. S. ROSE, of this city.

On the 13th inst, in Pike county, by the Rev. J. B. HANSON, MR. HENRY JOHNSTON, of Randolph, to MISS SARAH WILLIAMS, of Pike county.

In Jones county, on the evening of the 18th inst, by WM. MORELAND, Esq., MR. JASPER F. GREER of Barnesville, to MISS MARY A. TOWNSEND of the former place.

Died – In Vineville on the morning of the 24th inst, after a lingering and painful illness WILLIAM SCOTT, Esq. in the 55th year of his age.

Died – In Knoxville, Ga. of Typhoid Fever, on the 20th inst. SIMEON ARTEMUS, infant son of GEORGE T. and ANN WALKER, aged 9 months and 11 days.

Issue of March 4, 1851

Married – In this city, on the 25th ult. By Rev. S. LANDRUM, MISS MARTHA D. MARTIN to Col. JOHN F. LAWSON, of Burke county.

In Houston county, on Thursday morning, the 26th ult., by the Rev. JAS. E. EVANS, DR. S. D. BRANTLY, of Washington and MISS MARY E. daughter of SAM'L DINKINS, Esq., formerly of Macon, Ga.

Died – In Oglethorpe county, Ga., on the 19th ult. And in the 24th year of her age, MRS. NAOMI LANDRUM, wife of Rev. SYLVANUS LANDRUM, and daughter of the late Rev. JACK LUMPKIN.

Runaway – From the subscribers in Stewart county, on the night of the 16th inst., two negro men. They were brought from Mecklenberg county, North Carolina, and will probably endeavor to make their way back; their names are TOM and JIM, the latter is about 28 years old, yellow complexion, over six feet high and weighs about 170 lbs, has a dejected countenance and very slow in conversation. TOM is a large heavy built negro weighing about 180 lbs., about five feet eight or ten inches in height, yellow complexion, he is also quite slow in speech. We will give a liberal reward for the apprenhension and confinement of the above boys in some jail, or any information that will lead to their recovery. Address JAMES PERKINS and URIAH SENN, Greenville Post Office, Stewart co., Ga.

Issue of March 11, 1851

Married – On the 4th inst., at the residence of her father, ROLAND BIVINS, Esq. in Bibb county, by the Rev. W. H. ELLISON, MISS MARY F. BIVINS, to JESSE C. JACKSON, Esq. of Sumter counter.

On the morning of the 4th inst., by the Rev. JAS. E. EVANS, NELSON H. EDDY to MISS GEORGIANNA BEVERLY, daughter of R. B. WASHINGTON, Esq. all of this city.

In Bibb county, on the 10th inst., by Rev. S. LANDRUM, Col. NILO B. PARKER of Alabama to MISS SARAH ANN PERCY.

Died – In this county, on the 22d ult. of consumption, MR. JAMES H. AMASON, aged about 32 (?) years.

On the 23d ult., at the residence of her son, HENRY W. TISDALL (?), MRS ELIZABETH HUET, in the 74th year of her age, after a short but severe illness of Palsy.

In Carrollville, Tishomingo county, Mississippi, on the 7th ult., WILEN BELSHER, (difficult to read) near 60 years of age, formerly of Twiggs county, Ga.

Issue of March 18, 1851

Married – At Oak Bowery, Ala., on the 6th ult., by the Rev. JOHN STARR, ROBERT A. SMITH, Esq. of Macon, Ga., to MISS CATHERINE A. DOWDELL, of Chambers county, Ala.

In Wilkinson county, Ga., by Rev. JOHN EVANS, MR. JAMES VICKERS of Laurens to MISS ELIZABETH REBECCA BOSTWICK of Wilkinson.

Died – In Upson county, on the 13th inst., MR. MARTIN GAVAN, in the 44th year of his age. MR. GAVAN resided several years in this city, and by his steady and unobtrusive conduct won the esteem of all that knew him.

Issue of March 25, 1851

Death of Captain HENRY M. SHREVE – The St. Louis Republican, of the 7th inst. announces the death of this pioneer of steamboat navigation. He commanded the first steamer that ever ascended the Mississippi river. Whilst the British were threatening New Orleans in 1814 – 15, he was employed by Gen. JACKSON in several hazardous enterprises, and during the battle of January, served one of the field pieces which destroyed the advancing columns led by Gen. KEAN.

Death of Maj. W. S. HENRY – This distinguished officer of the U. S. Army, who contributed in no small degree to shed luster on our arms in the Mexican campaign, expired at New York, a few days since, in the 34th year of his age.

Died – On the evening of the 14th inst., of Inflammatory Rheumatism, after a painful illness of some days, CHARLES, the fourth son of MR. and MRS. GREER HILL, of Houston county, aged nine years ten months and twenty-eight days.

$10 Reward – Ranaway from the subscriber on the morning of the 22d inst., a negro man named CAIN, a heavy well built boy about 18 years old, about five feet 1 or 2 inches high, has a small scar in his forehead, had on a striped cotton shirt and Kentucky Jeans Pantaloons, had no coat or shoes when he left. I will give the above reward for his apprehension & delivery to me. It is probable he will make his way to Savannah.

ELIAS JENKINS

Issue of April 1, 1851

Death of Gen. BROOKE – The New Orleans Picayune of the 19th ult., says: We regret to learn from Captain LAWLESS, of the steamship Louisiana, which vessel arrived in port yesterday, from Matagorda Bay and Galveston, that an express arrived at Indianola just as the Louisiana was leaving, bringing intelligence of the death of Gen. BROOKE. He died at San Antonio on the 6th inst. We can only hope that the report will prove untrue, though we scarcely see room for doubt.

Of the military history of this distinguished officer the following particulars, taken from the Washington National Intelligencer, cannot at this moment be uninteresting to any soldier: Gen. BROOKE entered the army, from Virginia, on the 3d of May 1808, as First Lieutenant in the 5th Infantry. He was promoted to the rank of Captain the 1st of May, 1810; to that of Major of the 4th Infantry in 1814; to that of Lieut. Colonel same regiment March of 1819; and in July 1831, to the rank of Colonel in the 5th Infantry. His first brevet was that of Lieut. Colonel, August 15, 1814, for the gallant conduct in the defense of Fort Erie; his second was that of Colonel, September 17, 1814, for distinguished and meritorious services in the sortie from Fort Erie. He was made a Brevet Brigadier General, September 1, 1824, for ten years faithful service as Colonel; and he was brevetted a Major General, May 30th 1848, for meritorious conduct, particularly in the performance of his duties in the prosecution of the war with Mexico. Fort Brooke, at Tampa Bay, was established by him and received his name, in 1824, where he was stationed for a number of years. At the time of his death, he was in command of the 8th military department, (Texas) and engaged in planning an expedition against the Indians.

An American Citizen Imprisoned in France – MR. WILLIAM E. PETTY, a native born citizen of the United States, writes home to his friends that he has been incarcerated for fifteen months past in the prison of Paimboof, in France, on a charge of which he is entirely innocent, and that he has had no assistance from the American Consul, MR. ROQUES, at Nantes, whose duty it was to extend to him all the protection in his power. What MR. PETTY's offence was does not appear, but as the Consul has been thus publicly accused, the latter will doubtless communicate to Government the facts in the case.

Affray at a University – Student Shot by a Tutor. At the Missouri University , in Columbia, Mo., a serious affray took place. GEORGE P. CLARKSON, a student, took offence at ROBERT A. GRANT, a Tutor, for informing the faculty of some offence of his. He accordingly chastised him in the street, and the faculty then expelled him. On the afternoon of the 4th inst., CLARKSON attacked GRANT with a stick in one hand and a pistol in the other, and GRANT, drawing a pistol, fired first, the ball entering CLARKSON'S left side. CLARKSON fired first without inflicting any injury, GRANT surrendered himself to the authorities.

Death of Judge BROOKE – The Fredericksburg, (Va.) News announces the death of the venerable FRANCIS J.

38

BROOKE, in the eighty-eighth year of his age. He died at his residence, in Spotsylvania county, on the 3d ult. He was aide-de-camp to Gen. WASHINGTON, and for fifty years a Judge of the Court of Appeals of the State of Virginia.

A negro, belonging to MR. READING, of New Orleans, while at a ball on READING'S plantation, a short distance back of Warrenton, struck MR. STRONG, the overseer of the plantation with an axe. MR. STRONG died at 8 o'clock this morning, in consequence of the blow. At the time of the occurrence, STRONG was endeavoring to force admittance into the house where the ball was going forward. The negro was brought to Vicksburg, where he was confined in the jail.

Died – In Bibb county, on the 28th ult., DAVID F. RILEY, Senr., in the 55th year of his age.

Sudden Death of a Distinguished Lawyer. AUGUSTUS MOORE, Esq., a distinguished member of the North Carolina Bar, and formerly a Superior Court Judge in that State, died suddenly at his residence in Edenton on Sunday night last. MR. MOORE was apparently in good health and while sitting in his house was seized with an apoplectic fit and died in a few minutes. Norfolk Herald

Married – On Wednesday evening, the 2d last, by Rev. R. HOOKER, PROF. JOHN T. COXE of the Southern B.M. College, to MISS JEMIMA J. MCMULLAN, of this city.

In Lowndes county, Ga., on the 30th March, by E. C. DUKES, Esq., MR. ROBERT M. D. PEACOCK to MISS PENELOPE GRAHAM sixth daughter of MRS. MARY and the late ALEXANDER GRAHAM, Esq., of Telfair county.

Died – Of Typhoid Fever, at the residence of his relative, MR. C. M. LUCAS, in Crawford county, on the 19th ult.,

MR. JOHN L. DUGGER, in the 36th year of his age. He leaves a large circle of relatives and friends to mourn his early death.

Issue of April 15, 1851

THOMAS PITT, who recently murdered TILMAN HOYT (?), a slave dealer, near Fayettville, N. C. and afterwards fled to the North, and for whose apprehension the Governor of N. C. offered a reward of $100, has been arrested in New York. He passed through Richmond a few days since in the custody of a couple of police officers. Richmond Enquirer

Died – In this city, on the 1st of April, after an illness of 13 days, of Scarlet Fever, RYLAND JUDSON, son of LEWIS J. and MARGARET GROCE, aged 3 years, one month and two days.

Issue of April 22, 1851

Death of GEORGE SCHLEY, Esq. – The Savannah papers of Friday last, announce the death of GEORGE SCHLEY, Esq., late Postmaster, in that city, on the day previously. MR. S. was a native of Jefferson county in this State, but early in life removed to Savannah, where he has resided for the last forty-five years.

The Son of Marshal JUNOT – Another name has been added to the obituary of the distinguished persons of the present year. NAPOLEON JUNOT of
Abrantes, the elder of the two sons who survived the Marshal, has just died, in the 44th year of his age, in a lunatic asylum near Paris.

MISS HARRIET W. (daughter of the late Prof. WEBSTER) was married at

Cambridge, Mass. On the 2d inst., to MR. S. W. DABNEY of Fayal, the brother of her elder sister's husband. When her father was convicted of the murder of DR. PARKMAN, this young lady, who had been for some time betrothed to MR. D. absolved him from his engagement, which, however with a manliness that did him honour, he would not accept. They, with MRS. WEBSTER are about making a visit to Fayal.

Married – In this city on the morning of the 17th, by the Rev. J. A. SHANKLIN, Rector of Christ's Church, MR. JAMES R. KING, of Roswell, to MISS ELIZABETH FRANCES, youngest daughter of the late OLIVER H. PRINCE.

Issue of April 29, 1851

Judge HENRY A. BULLARD, member elect, to fill the vacancy occasioned in the Second Congressional District of Louisiana, by the entrance of MR. CONRAD into the cabinet of MR. FILLMORE, died at New Orleans on the 17th inst.

Married – In this city, on the 23d inst, by the Rev. MR. EVANS, MR. ALBERT G. BOSTICK, to MISS AURELIA L., second daughter of DR. T. B. GORMAN.

Issue of May 20, 1851

Married – In Warrenton, on the 27th ult., MR. WILLIAM W. HAMMOND, of Elberton, to MISS ANN E. J. BLOUNT, of Warren co., Ga.

Died – At the residence of her husband, in this county, on the 10th inst., MRS. RACHEL B., wife of MR. L. B. AVANT.

In this city, on the 12th inst., in her 25th year, MRS. MARY, wife of JACKSON BARNES.

Issue of May 27, 1851

HORACE WELLS, the type founder, of Cincinnati, being up at Oxford, Ohio, on the 12th, was accidentally shot dead in the street, by the careless _____of a rifle by a medical student, named DR. BOYCE, inside of a hotel nearby. Another young man had just come in and laid the rifle down, when DR. BOYCE took it up.

A Duel – Lieut. ADAMS and Lieut. EDWARDS, Third Artillery, stationed at Fort Moultrie, S. C., have had a hostile meeting at Sullivan's Island. After an exchange of shots, by which EDWARDS was slightly wounded in the back, the difficulty was reconciled. A lady, we believe, was at the bottom of the misunderstanding, as usual.

Died – In this city, on the 24th inst., MRS. CATHARINE A., consort of ROBT. A. SMITH, Esq.

Married – On the evening of the 26th inst., by Rev. MR. BIVINS, MR. T. A. GOODWIN, to MISS CORINTHIA A. daughter of the late Major LUKE J. MORGAN, of this city.

Issue of June 3, 1851

Married – In Mobile, on the 22nd ult., by Rev. MR. MELBOURNE, Col. JOHN J. RAWLS, of this city, to MISS M. S. DENT, first daughter of Gen. D. DENT of Mobile.

Died – On Monday, 19th ult., LEWIS NEALE, infant son of MR. and MRS. L. N. WHITTLE, aged 7 months and 1 day.

Issue of June 10, 1851

Married – In this city, on Thursday evening last, by the Hon. KEELIN COOK, MR. LAWSON G. PUCKETT of Macon to MISS HANNAH MERIDITH of Philadelphia.

In Griffin, on the 28th ult., by Rev. W. J. KEITH, MR. JOSHUA CHERRY, of Macon to MRS. SARAH MCDONALD of Griffin.

Died – In this city, on Thursday last, ALEXANDER, only child of FRANCIS S. and DOLORES HERNANDEZ, aged one year and six months.

Issue of June 17, 1851

Duel – We learn from the Savannah papers of Wednesday last, that an affair of honor came off the day previous, on the opposite side of the Savannah river, between MESSRS. WM. H. MONGIN and CHARLES ARNOLD of that city. The weapons were rifles – distance thirty paces. After an exchange of two shots without injury to either party, upon the interferance of friends, the difficulty was amicably adjusted, and the parties returned to the city.

Hon. W. C. DAWSON – The friends of Senator DAWSON will regret to learn that he had a leg severly fractured on the 10th inst. The following letter from a gentleman in Greensboro,to a friend in Savannah, furnishes the particulars. Dear Sir:
The Hon. WM. C. DAWSON, while at his plantation this morning, had his left leg badly fractured above the ankle, which will doubtless confine him to his room for weeks. He had just dismounted and tied his horse to the top rail of the fence, when the horse became frightened and ran with the rail fastened to the bridle, and in passing, Judge D. was struck by the rail, which caused the injury. He is now suffering much, though doing very well.

Married – On Thursday evening last, by the Rev. MR. HOOKER, MR. WILLIAM BAILEY, of St. Mary's Ga., to MISS MARTHA J. HADAWAY, of this city.

On Wednesday evening, 11th inst., by the Rev. JOHN E. DAWSON, Col. W. I. LAWTON, of Scriven county to MISS SARAH E. daughter of MR. N. R. LEWIS, of Russel county, Ala.

In Leon county, Fla., on the 3d inst., by the Rev. SAMUEL WOODBURY, MR. EDWIN SAULSBURY, of this city to MISS ELMINA CHAIRS, daughter of GREEN H. CHAIRS.

Near Columbus, Ga., on the 27th ult., EVERAND H. ABERCROMBIE to MISS PAULINE, daughterof the late Judge NICHOLAS LEWIS of Lagrange.

In Columbus, Ga., on the 29th ult., by the Rev. MR. BARBER, DR. J. A. LAMAR to MISS LUCINDA S. CALLAWAY of Montgomery, Ala.

In Columbus, Ga., on the 29th ult., by the Rev. MR. BARKS, MR. N. T. GREEN to MISS LAURA C. TICKNER of Montgomery, Ala.

Obituary – Death of CHARLES S. HAWLEY. A native of Pennsylvania, and reared and educated in Philadelphia...About ten years ago he came to Georgia...admitted to the bar in 1843... He located in Hawkinsville in the county of Pulaski...In1848, he married a daughter of Col. DAVID C. CAMPBELL and in 1850 removed to this city...He expired at his residence in this city, on the evening of the 5th instant.

Died – In this city,on Monday, 13th inst., SARAH BULLOCK, youngest daughter of HENRY G. ROSS, Esq., aged 27 months.

In Vineville, 14th inst., BENJAMIN JONES, infant son of Col. N. J. and V. B. LAMAR, aged 4 months.

At the residence of his mother, in Jones county, on Wednesday, 11th June, Capt. ROBERT M. BROACH, formerly of this city, aged 38 years and 1 month.

In Sparta, Ga. on the 23d ult., RICHARD P. SARSNETT (?), Esq. in the 39(?)th year of his age, after a protracted illness of several months...He left a wife and five children to mourn their irreparable loss.

Died – At Indian Springs, Butts county, on the 7th inst., MRS. VALINDA, wife of DR. H. BRANHAM, of Eatonton, Putnam county.

Obituary – Departed this life, in Crawford co. Ga., on the 15th ult. MRS. JANE FRANCIS CRUTCHFIELD, consort of HILLARD CRUTCHFIELD, Esq. in the 27th year of her age...a bereaved husband...and four young and tender little boys...a fond and tender mother...

Issue of July 1, 1851

Arrest of W. S. BROWN - There were some circumstances attending the arrest of W. S. BROWN who was taken to Washington on Wednesday last, by the U. S. Marshall, CHARLES H. KNOX, which deserve to be adverted to. BROWN had been traveling through the Southwest, and was expected to be at Detroit about this time. Just before his arrival a letter was received at the Detroit Post Office for W. S. BROWN; this letter fell into the hands of a gentleman having the same name and initials, who, upon opening it, found that it contained a warning from a friend in Washington, that a bill of indictment was ready against him for the offence of dealing in false or fraudulent land warrants; the information having of course been communicated to Hon. GEORGE C. BATES, U. S. District Attorney, he telegraphed to Washington, and in answer learned that BROWN was so indicted. Soon after the receipt of the letter, and the disclosure, BROWN made his

45

appearance, when he was taken by the Marshal, and the next day carried to Washington. BROWN professed ignorance of the whole transition and with great sang froid assured the Marshal "that it was quite unnecessary for him to go to Washington, as he was himself about to visit that city, and to demand an immediate investigation." Marshal KNOX, fearing he might not possibly take the most direct route, determined to accompany him, "just", as he said, "to see that he did not get lost." Detroit Daily Adv. Of 10th

Married – On the 12th inst. by the Rev. W. W. HARDY, at the residence of DR. S.W. BURNEY, in Monroe county, Ga., AMBROSE CHAPMAN, Esq. to MISS E. A. FREEMAN.

Obituary – Died in the city of Macon, on the 21st instant, MRS. MARY E., wife of JAS. VAN VALKENBURGH, in the 41st year of her age...She was the eldest daughter of NATHAN CHURCH, Esq., of Troy, N. Y. and was born in the year 1810. Her parents were Baptists; and both died before she was fifteen years of age. She then became the ward of ISRAEL SEYMORE, Esq., her uncle...She married JAS. VAN VALKENBURGH, in 1827; In 1833, she made a public profession of religion – joined the Church under the pastoral care of the Rev. D. DUNBAR, of New York City, and of which church her husband was a member. In uniting with the Church, she dated her conversion back to her fourteenth year, near the time of her father's death. Subsequently, the family changed their membership to16th St. Baptist Church, where her membership remained until her death. In 1847, she removed to Macon, Ga. enjoying improved health, until within two weeks of her death. During this illness, from Dysentery, her sufferings were undescribable...

Died – In Crawford county, Ga. on Monday evening, 23d inst, JAMES EDWARD, son of CHARLES H. and

CAROLINE E. WALKER, aged three years and eight months.

Issue of July 8, 1851

Death of BENJAMIN BURGOYNE – (Article difficult to read).

Died – In Savannah, on the morning of the 24th June, DR. JOHN V. MITCHELL, (late a resident of New Orleans) in the 34th year of his age. DR. M. was a native of St. Stevens, New Brunswick, and had arrived in Savannah a few weeks previous, intending to locate there, for the purpose of carrying on his professional business – he has left a disconsolate wife to mourn his loss.

Issue of July 15, 1851

Married – In Baker county, on the 10th inst., by Rev. MR. KETCHENS, MR. SHADRACH ATKINSON, to MISS ELIZABETH PERKINS.

On the 9th inst., by the Hon. LOTT WARREN, MR. HUGH THOMPSON, to MISS FRANCIS R. HARVEY.

Died – In the city of London, on the 5th ult., EDWARD A. BRODDUS, M. D. of Monticello, Jasper county, Georgia, in the 50th year of his age.

Issue of August 5, 1851

Married – In Woodville, Ga., on the 20th ult., by WM. C. GREER, Esq., Col. FREDERICK L. STOREY, to MISS MARTHA JANE, daughter of F. WATSON, Esq., all of Dooly co.

On the 24ᵗʰ ult., by P. SHOUSE, Esq., MR. WILLIAM T. STARKE, of Russell county, Ala., to MISS MARGARET A. MARKS, of Morgan county, Ga.

Issue of August 12, 1851

Married – On the 2d inst., by Rev. RICHARD HOOKER, DAVIS (?) SMITH, JR., and MISS ROSETTA A. HOLLINGSWORTH, all of this city.

Obituary – Departed this life, on the morning of the 1ˢᵗ of August, 1851, at the residence of his uncle, JOHN NEAL, in Zebulon, DAVID N. VARNER, Esq., in the 41ˢᵗ year of his age. Disease (kidney affection) selected him…He was for the last six months confined to his room under medical treatment…The deceased resided in Zebulon for the last 25 years of his life…

Issue of August 19, 1851

Married – On the 6ᵗʰ inst., in Columbus, Ga., by the Rev. J. CRUMLEY, MR. HENRY W. VERSTILLE, of Savannah, Ga., to MISS ELLEN J. youngest daughter of DR. HENRY LOCKHART, of Columbus, Ga.

In Atlanta, on the 24ᵗʰ ult., by the Rev. MR. JOHNSON, MR. DAVID A. COOK, formerly of Macon, to MISS NANCY W., daughter of MERIL COLLIER, Esq., of the former place.

Died – In this city, on Sunday morning last, JOHN, only son of JOHN W. and HARRIET A. BABCOCK, of Macon – aged 7 months and 22 days.

In Oglethorpe, Ga., on the 11ᵗʰ inst., after an illness of 18 days with Typhoid Fever, MR. REUBEN A. SMITH formerly of Coweta county, but for the last 8 or 10 months a resident of Oglethorpe.

Issue of August 26, 1851

Died – On the 17th inst. at the residence of his uncle, the Hon. WM. H. STILES, in Cass county, MR. JOSEPH STILES, late of Savannah; son of BENJ. E. STILES, of Macon, in the 27th year of his age.

At her residence in Talbot county, on the 16th inst., MRS. ELIZABETH P. DUNCAN, wife of FRANKLIN DUNCAN, in the 32d year of her age. The deceased was a devoted member of the Methodist church...She has left a husband, two little daughters, a step daughter, and an extensive family relation to mourn her loss.

Issue of September 9, 1851

Death of an Editor – We regret to observe in the North Carolinian, published in Fayetteville, N. C. the announcement of the death of its editor, WM. H. BAYNE, Esq. who died on the 22d inst. The deceased was a native of Washington City, but had been a resident of Fayetteville since the 4th of July, 1840, at which time he took charge of the Carolinian.

To Be Married Again – a letter from Kentucky, says that SALLIE WARD, the queen of western beauty, who was once MRS. LAWRENCE, is soon again to be led to the altar. The happy individual who is about to take sweet NELLIE by the hand is DR. HUNT, a near relative of HENRY CLAY.

Died – In Bibb county, on the 21st ult., MR. ADAM ROBINSON, aged about 80 years. MR. R. was one of the earliest settlers of this vicinity...

On the 30th ultimo, at his residence near Jackson, Butts county, Ga. after an illness of seventeen days, MR. JAMES A. MCCUNE, aged 60 years.

In Griffin, on the 29th ult., DR. NATHAN B. JOHNSON, a worthy and highly respectable citizen of this place. DR. JOHNSON was about 30 years of age...and was at his demise, a candidate for a seat in the State Legislature.

Issue of September 16, 1851

Gen. JOHN PRAGAY – We learn from the New Orleans Delta, that this gallant and accomplished gentleman and soldier, who went with Gen. LOPEZ, as Chief of his staff, was killed in the second action of Las Pozas. Gen. PRAGAY was Adjutant General under KLAPHA, at Comorn, when that last stronghold of the Hungarians made an honorable capitulation. He was about forty years of age, of commanding appearance and most pleasing address. As a soldier, full of ardor and the spirit of enterprise, as well as skilled in all military duties, he had few superiors. From the time of his arrival in New Orleans, he became an intimate friend of Gen. LOPEZ, and had arranged to accompany him in the expedition composed chiefly of Hungarians which was frustrated last spring. Gen. PRAGAY was a native of Pesth, Hungary. He was the author of an interesting work on the Hungarian War, which contained some valuable biographies of the leading men of that war.

Married – On the 2d inst., by Rev. J. A. SHANKLIN, WM. B. JOHNSON, Esq. to MISS ANN E. TRACY, eldest daughter of the late Judge TRACY.

50

Issue of September 23, 1851

Death of BEVERLY TUCKER – We are pained (says the Southern Press) to announce the death of BEVERLY TUCKER, Esq., late professor of law in William and Mary College.

The lady of the Attorney General of the United States, MRS. CRITTENDEN, died at Frankfort, Kentucky on the 8th inst.

The Fugitive Slave Law – A new fugitive case occurred in Buffalo, New York, a few days ago. A fugitive slave named DANIEL, belonging to a gentleman in Kentucky, was arrested on the affidavit of the agent of his master, and the commissioner before whom he was taken, directed him to be given up. But the district judge of the United States, CONKLING, granted a writ of habeas corpus, and discharged him from custody on the ground, that the provisions of the law were prospective, and did not apply to those fugitives who had escaped before its passage, as was the case in this instance.

Married – In Jones county, on the 11th inst., by THOMAS L. BURDEN, Esq., JAMES C. WOOP, Esq. to MISS ELIZABETH SHARP, daughter of JAMES SHARP, Esq. all of Jones county.

Died – In this city, on the 13th inst., after a short illness, MRS. CATHERINE M. STOW, aged 27 years – wife of JOHN B. STOW, and daughter of the late FREDERICK SIMS, Esq.

Issue of September 30, 1851

Married – In Atlanta on the 23d inst., by the Rev. WM. J. ZIMMER, MR. ALLMAND A. MCCOY of Clinton, N. C. to

MISS S. ANOIEUX, daughter of the late Rev. JOHN HOWARD.

Died – On the Steam ship Alabama, bound to New York on Monday morning 15th inst., MRS. S. E. H. LOOMIS, wife of Prof. J. N. LOOMIS of Marietta, Ga.

Issue of October 14, 1851

Fatal Affray in Baker county – The Albany Patriot the 3d inst., states that a misunderstanding and recounter occurred on the Wednesday previously, between DR. J. G. BYRD and Maj. N. .C. JONES, which resulted in the death of the latter. The affair is undergoing legal investigation.

Hon. JAMES GRAHAM, the second son of the late JOSEPH GRAHAM, and the last surviving brother of the Secretary of the Navy, died at Li_bo_, N. C.

Died – In Macon, on the 29th ult., BASIL L. LUNSFORD, aged eleven years.

In Grantland, on the 28th ult., MRS. SARAH GOODWIN, in the 91st year of her age.

In Scotsboro, on the 26th ult., MRS. CATHARINE FURMAN, wife of DR. FURMAN, and daughter of Col. FARISH CARTER.

In Jones county, on the 29th ult., MR. JOHN M. BROACH in the 35th year of his age.

Married Again – MISS SALLIE WARD, late MRS. LAURENCE, is reported to have been married on the 1st inst., at the residence of her father, at Louisville, Ky. To DR. ROBERT P. HUNT.

Issue of October 21, 1851

Married – In Houston county, on the 8th inst., by the Rev. MR. ADAM HOLMES, EDWARD L. FELDER, Esq., and MISS ADA THARPE.

Died – In this city, on the 3d inst., MISS SUSAN SIMS, relict of the late FREDERICK SIMS, in the 51st year of her age.

In Vineville on the 13th inst., JOSEPH A. OUSLEY, infant son of ROBERT F. and E. D. OUSLEY, aged 17 months and 7 days.

Issue of October 28, 1851

Married – In Pike county, Ga., near Barnesville, on the 19th inst., by Judge WILLIAM O. KENDRICK, MR. J. B. MOYE, to MISS MARY E. BRANTLEY, daughter of SIMEON BRANTLEY, Esq. of Meriwether county, Ga.

Five Dollars Reward – I have every reason to think that my girl, CAROLINE, is in and around the vicinity of Macon. She professes to be hired out at work. She is a very fine looking girl, with a full face, and a fine head of hair; generally well combed, and when at home, dresses well.

C. TAYLOR

Issue of November 4, 1851

Married – In this city, on the 30th ult., by the Rev. R. HOOKER, Gen. SAMUEL R. CHANDLER, of Sumter District, S. C. to MISS MARY JACQUE BURCH.

Issue of November 18, 1851

Convictions in the U. S. Court – In the U. S. Circuit Court yesterday, a young man named ROBERT MELTON, about 17 years of age, and a native of Alabama, was tried for stealing from the U. S. mail, a letter containing a draft of $62. There were three counts in the indictment, and the jury found him guilty on the third, which charged him with stealing from the mail. He was a mail rider between Darien and Hawkinsville in this State.

On Tuesday last, H. L. KIMBROUGH, of Columbus, in this State, was tried, charged with imbezzling six thousand dollars from the post office in Columbus, some time in December last. The jury found him guilty. At a previous term of the Court, this young man was tried but the jury did not agree on the verdict.

Married – On Monday evening the 5th inst., by JOHN SWINT, Esq., MR. BARTLEY M. C. BATEMAN, of Houston county to MISS CATHERINE H. POOL, OF Washington county.

Died – In this city, on the 15th inst. after a brief illness: MR. JOHN EANES, a native of Virginia, but for the last fourteen years a resident of Macon, in the sixty-second year of his age.

In this city on the 1`5th inst. in the 36th year of his age, DANIEL D. MCNEILL, a native of Person county, N. C. but for the last thirteen years a resident of this city.

Issue of November 25, 1851

Married – On the afternoon of the 11th inst., by the Rev. DR. BARRY of Augusta, THOMAS C. DEMPSEY, Esq. of Macon and MISS MARIA LOUISA, daughter of Col. AUGUSTUS ALDEN of Marietta.

Died – At Americus Friday 21st inst. of Typhoid Fever, MR. LEANDER M. HUDSON, in the 29th year of his age. MR. HUDSON, in the 29th year of his age. MR. HUDSON was a native of Laurens county and had removed to the city of Oglethorpe where he resided at the time his death. He had visited Albany, Baker county and was returning to Oglethorpe; and on reaching Americus became too ill to travel and after a lingering illness of 51 days died in the prime of manhood...his devotion to his brothers and sisters...

Died – At his residence in Twiggs county, on the 19th inst., Gen H. H. TARVER in the 61st year of his age.

Issue of December 2, 1851

During the sitting of the Court at Marion Court-house, N. C. while Col. W. W. AVERY, was passing from the Court house to his room, he was attacked by a man named SAMUEL FLEMING who had armed himself, and used a cow-hide on the person of Col. AVERY. The parties were then separated. Subsequently, during the sitting of the Court in Morgantown, FLEMING fully armed walked within the bar of the Court, appearing for the first time, since the attack with the cow-hide, in the presence of Col. AVERY, whereupon AVERY arose and shot FLEMING dead on the spot, the ball passing through his heart. Col. AVERY at once placed himself in the custody of the proper officer, and has since been tried and acquitted.

$25 Reward – Runaway from the subscriber in Bibb county, Georgia, on the night of the 29th November last, nine miles South of Macon, a Negro boy, named CANE, about five feet six inches high, 18 or 20 years old, well set, rather of copper color, with a fierce quick countenance, with good sense, pretty well dressed. I expect that he will make his way to Hawkinsville or Savannah, as he has done so before. I am told he has a brother in Hawkinsville, and father in Savannah. He rode off a common sized black horse, with a fistula, which as lately been on the left side of his weathers; he paces and trots well, about 10 or 12 years old. The above reward will be paid to any person that will deliver the said negro to me or I will liberally compensate any person that will confine him in jail so that I can get him. Any person that will deliver me the horse, will be amply rewarded, or any information thankfully received.

WM. R. BUSBY

Issue of December 16, 1851

Married – In this city, on the 30th ult., by the Rev. J. E. EVANS, MR. ALEXANDER A. MENARD, to MISS CAROLINE RICHARDS, both of this city.

In Eatonton, on the 26(?)th ult., by the Rev. M. E. HEBBARD, DR. PRICE S. GAITHER, of Oxford, Ga., to MISS ELIZABETH JARRATT, of the former place.

In Eatonton, on the 4th inst., by the Rev. S. C. HAMBLETON, MR. D. A. CRAWFORD, to MISS SARAH E., daughter of MR. SAMUEL MCDOW, all of Cass county.

In Early county, on the 13th ult., by L. Q. C. FRANKLIN, Esq., MR. JAMES S. ROWLAND, of Fort Gaines(?), to MRS. ANN JANE MCLEAN.

In Fort Gaines, on the 27th ult., by L. Q. C. FRANKLIN, Esq. MR. _ASTON G. BASS to MISS M. E. BRADLEY.

Died – In this city, on the 11th inst., MR. RUFUS ___ EVANS, aged 53 years Rochester (?), New Hampshire.

In Washington county, Texas, on the 13(?)th ult., COLLIER FOSTER, in the 61st year of his age. He was formerly a citizen of Monroe county, Ga. and removed to Texas during the fall of 1850. He was born in Columbia county, Ga.

In Crawford county, on the 4(?)th inst., after a protracted illness, Maj. WILLIS BOON, in the 66th year of his age.

In Marietta, on the 4th inst., Gen. JOHN S. ANDERSON, after a painful and protracted illness.

Issue of December 23, 1851

Married – In Monroe county, on the 18th inst., by the Rev. J. C. SIMMONS, MR. WILLIAM WILLIAMS, of Pike county, to MISS MARY A. BLOUNT, of Monroe county.

Died – In Houston county, on the 11th ult., after a few days illness, FLORA, daughter of MURDOCK and ELIZA A. M. CASKILL, aged 10 months and 17 days.

In Jasper county, on the 27th ult., MR. GEORGE CLARK, a Revolutionary soldier, in the 92d year of his age. MR. CLARK was a native of Virginia, and shortly after the declaration of peace, emigrated to this State, where he has ever since resided. He was an upright and faithful citizen, a kind and obliging neighbor, and for forty years a pious and exemplary member of the Methodist Episcopal Church.

In Savannah, on the 17th inst., HENRY R. DEADWYLER, Esq., a member of the Legislature from Elbert county.

Death of the Hon. JOEL R.(?) POINSETT – It is with deep and sincere regret that we announce the death of this eminent citizen and retired statesman in the 73d year of his age. A private letter, received in this city, states that he died at Statesburg, on the 12th inst. MR. POINSETT was born in this city, on the 2d March, 1779... (From the Charleston Mercury)

Issue of December 30, 1851

Death of WILLIAM PITT

Married – In Crawford county, on the 23d of October last, by M. C. H. WALKER, J. P., MR. JAMES M. JACKSON to MISS NANCY ANN ELIZABETH BRASWELL.

In Crawford county, on the 23d ult., by C. H. WALKER, J. P. MR. WILLIAM BUNDRICK, to MISS JUDY SPILLAR.

In Crawford county, on the 18th inst., by C. H. WALKER, J. P., MR. GEORGE DRAYTON MATHEWS, to MISS ELIZA MISSOURIE FELTS.

In Crawford county, on the 21st inst., by C. H. WALKER, J. P., MR. MOSES MATTHEWS,to MISS MARY ANN ROBERTS.

Ten Dollars Reward – If caught in Florida or near the Georgia line, or Twenty-five Dollars Reward if caught in Middle or Upper Georgia. Runaway from the subscriber on the 13th inst., his negro man, JOHNSON, a likely black fellow, about 20 years of age, 5 feet 6 or 8 inches in height, rather stout, with a bluff manner of expressing himself, a small crown, and good teeth, not very square in front. The above reward will be paid for his lodgment in any secure jail where I man get him. He came in the beginning of this year from near Pendleton, S. C. and has relatives near that place, and has probably gone there through Middle and Upper Georgia, though he may still be in Florida. Any communication addressed to me, directed "Anzie Island, Pilatka P. O., East Florida", will receive prompt attention.

J. C. CALHOUN, per F. M. ADAMS

Ten Dollars Reward – Ranaway from the subscriber on the 12th inst., his negro man, TOM. He is about 5 feet 10 inches high, tall, well made, and very likely, not very dark, smooth spoken, smooth skin. I think he may be lurking about Macon, or may have gotten some one to conduct him off. He has had a wife at Gen. RUTHERFORD'S in Houston. I will give the above reward for his apprehension and delivery to me in Monroe county, or to any jail, so that I may get him again; and if taken off by any white man $25 for the delivery of both.

THOMAS DYSON

Issue of January 6, 1852

Married – In Jones county, on the 11th ult., by the Hon. JAMES G. BARNES, MR. B. A. BUCKNER, of Putnam county, to MISS NANCY J. MESSER, of Jones county.

In Jones county, by the Hon. JAMES G. BARNES, MR. W. B. GOOLSBY, of Jasper county, to MISS ADELAIDE E. COOK, of Jones county.

In Butts county, on the 25th ult., by the Rev. MR. CARTER, MR. JOSEPH S. JOBSON, of Perry, to MISS ELIZABETH KEY, of the former place.

In Oglethorpe, on the 25th ult., by the Rev. P. S. J. MAY, MR. JOHN W. SULLIVAN, to MISS GEORGIA VIRGINIA HAWFIELD, both of this city.

Died – In Cass county, on the 4th ult., MRS. MARGARET L. B. WILLIAMS, wife of ALLEN A. WILLIAMS, and daughter of the Hon. JOHN M. BERRIEN.

Issue of January 13, 1852

Married – On the 11th inst., by Rev. S. LANDRUM, CHAS. G. BEAVERS, of Crawford county, to MISS CAMELLA J. SHEFFIELD, of Bibb.

Ranaway from the subscriber , on the 3d inst., a Negro man by the name of RALPH. It is supposed he is trying to make his way to North Carolina, where he was purchased last winter. He wore off a suit of Linsey clothes; sack coat, very large for him, and a wool hat considerably worn. RALPH is a dark copper colored man, 23 or 24 years old, about six feet high, weighs about 180 lbs, and is rather likely and intelligent. He has two scars on the left side of his face, one over the eye-lid and the other under it, which gives him the appearance of slightly squinting; the scar over the eye is about an inch long. Any person taking up the Negro and lodging him in Jail, and informing me of it, will be liberally rewarded.

NELSON TIFT

Married – In Bibb county, on the 15th inst., by the Rev. RICHARD A. CAIN, MR. SAMUEL H. EVERETT, of Atlanta, to MISS ADRION SUSAN LOUISA, youngest daughter of MR. AUGUSTIN COOK.

In Charleston, S. C. in the 12th inst., by the Rev. WHITFORD SMITH, ARTHUR FAIRLEY, to MYRA R. daughter of B. R. GITSINGER, Esq., all of that place.

Died – In this county, on the 9th inst., BENJAMIN MAY, Esq. in the 76 year of his age. MR. MAY, was native of Edgecomb county, N. C. and when quite young came with his father to this State, where he has resided ever since. He joined the Baptist Church early in life, and for the last thirty years has been a ruling Deacon in that denomination...

In Pulaski county, on the 4th inst., MRS. SUSAN T. MONK, in the 66th year of her age.

Issue of January 27, 1852

Married- In Pike county, on the 22d inst., by the Rev. J. B. HANSON, MR. THOMAS G. WILLIAMS, to MISS LUCINDA A. ALLEN, all of Pike county, Georgia.

Died – In this city, MR. BENJAMIN TRAPP, aged about fifty years.

Issue of February 3, 1852

Died – In Vineville on the morning of the 31st ult., at the residence of her daughter MRS. JEWETT, MRS. CHERRY MALONE, in the sixty-seventh year of her age.

Very suddenly, at his plantation, in Bibb county, on Wednesday night last, R. K. HINES, Esq., of this city, aged 46 years. Obituary notice next week.

Issue of February 10, 1852

The late Duel at Washington – The duel between the Editors of the Richmond Examiner and Whig – MESSRS DANIEL and JOHNSON, after the exchange of one shot on each side, was "honorably adjusted" in the presence of another Editor and quite a number of his distinguished gentlemen, "well capable", says the correspondent of the Baltimore Sun, "of judging honors cause". Good. So we have another "adjustment, and nobody hurt."
The duel was fought on the farm of F. P. BLAIR, near Washington City; and the parties, after the fun was over, shook hands, and then, by invitation of MR. BLAIR, went to his house and were entertained by him in his usual hospitable manner.

Marriage of JENNY LIND – The Telegraph announces the marriage of JENNY LIND, at Boston, on Thursday last, to OTTO GOLDSCHMIDT, the pianist.

Death of DR. RICHARDSONE – We regret to announce the death, in this city, at 4 o'clock this afternoon , of DR. COSMO P. RICHARDSONE, in the 48th year of his age. DR. R. was born in Edinburgh, Scotland, and came to Savannah when but three years old. He has resided here, we believe, ever since, and in the meantime, has amassed a handsome fortune, and established a reputation as a skilful physician and high-minded, honorable gentleman...

Died – Very suddenly, at his plantation, in Bibb county on Wednesday night last, the 28th ult., R. K. HINES, Esq. of this city, aged 46 years. The parents of MR. HINES emigrated from Virginia to Pittsboro, N. C. when his father died, and where he was born on the 15th day of October,

1805. His mother removed from thence, whilst he was still a child to Morgan county, Ga., and subsequently to Putnam county. He was graduated at Franklin College, in 1824, with the highest honor of his class and having studied law in the office of Judge L. Q. C. LAMAR, and opened an office in the city of Milledgeville, he was married on the 18th day of January, 1825, to a daughter of DR. JAMES NISBET, of Athens...he represented the county of Baldwin in the General Assembly of the Senate...

Married – In this city, on Thursday evening 5th inst., by the Rev. S. LANDRUM, MR. PULASKI S. HOLT, JR. to MISS JULIA MARIA DAVIS, daughter of DAVID J. DAVIS.

In Trinity Church, New Haven, Conn. On the 24th ult., by the Rev. MR. PITKIN, ALBERT MIX, Esq., of Macon, to MISS MARIA S. TOWNSEND, of the former city.

Issue of February 17, 1852

Died – In this city, on Monday morning, the 16th inst., after a short but painful illness, MR. DANIEL HEIDT, a native of Savannah, aged 43 years.

In Oglethorpe, on the morning of the 10th inst., MR. ROBERT P. ROBINSON, formerly for many years a merchant of this city.

Issue of February 1852

Death of JAMES G. BIRNEY – JAMES G. BIRNEY, who was, in 1844, the candidate of the "liberty Party" for President, died at Saginaw, Mich. a few days ago.

Married – On the evening of Tuesday last, near Milledgeville, by the Rev. JOHN W. BAKER, MR. JOSEPH H. NISBET, on the editors of the Federal Union, to MISS EMELIE M. DELAUNAY.

On the 1st instant, by DANIEL MCCOOK, Esq.MR. JAMES BECK and MISS SARAH CEARLING, all of Wilkinson county.

By the same, MR. JAMES G. JONES and MISS CAROLINE M. DAY, all of Wilkinson.

On Thursday the 19th inst., by the Rev. D. H. MOORE, MR. DAVID H. BENTON, to MISS NARCISSA P. BROWN, all of Monroe co., Ga.

On the 19th inst., by the Rev. S. LANDRUM, MR. D. W. ORR, of this city, to MISS LIZZIE SLAPPIE, OF Macon county, Ga.

Issue of March 2, 1852

Married – In Athens, on the 16th ult., by the Rev. DR. HOYT, Colonel PORTER KING, of Marion, Ala., to MISS CALLIE M. LUMPKIN, youngest daughter of Hon. JOSEPH H. LUMPKIN.

In Jackson county, on the 15th inst. by WILLIAM BELL, Esq. MR. WILLIAM G. LAVENDAR to MISS NANCE E. BOOTHE.

Died – In this city, on the night of 23d ult., after a short but severe illness, MR. JAMES A. DUDLEY, Printer, aged about 27 years, a native of Ithica, N. Y. MR. D. had resided in this city only about two months, and during the greater part of that time filled the situation of Foreman in this office. He was known to the craft in the cities of New York, Washington, Richmond, and Charleston, having spent some time in each of those places.

On Wednesday evening the 18th ult., MRS. MALINDA SHELTON, wife of MR. E. L. SHELTON, of this city, in the 28th year of her age.

Issue of March 9, 1852

Married – In Newton county, at the residence of DR. GEO. W. GRAVES, on the 4th inst., by the Rev. DR. PIERCE, Col. GEORGE WILLIAMSON of North Carolina, to MISS M. WALLACE HILL, formerly of North Carolina.

On the evening of the 12th ult., by the Rev. JAMES M. WOOD, Col. H. FIELDER, OF Van Wert, Ga., to MISS MARY BLANCE, of the same place.

Died – In Griffin, on the 27th ult., of typhoid pneumonia, MR. JOHN G. HILL, merchant of Griffin, in the 42d year of his age.

Death of WILLIAM B. BULLOCK – It is with deepest sorrow that we announce the death, in this city, at a quarter past one o'clock this afternoon, of the Hon. WILLIAM B. BULLOCK, in his 77th year. (long article).

Issue of March 16, 1852

Married – In Telfair county, on Sunday evening, the 29th February, by DUNCAN B. GRAHAM, J.I.C. RANDALL FOLSOM, Esq. of Lowdnes county, to MISS MENETTA F. GRAHAM of Telfair.

In Burke, March 7th, by the Rev. JOHN TUCKER, A.L. ARCHER, Esq. to MISS MARTHA M. second daughter of H. FLANDERS, Esq. of Macon, Ga.

At the house of W. C. RIDDLE, Esq. , on the 3d inst., by the Rev. J. P. LEVERETT, DR. JOHN C. STANCEL, of

Ala. To MISS SEANY ANN GILMORE, of Washington county.

On the 22d ult., by SAMUEL BEALL, Esq., MR. MATHEW CARSWELL, to MISS SARAH E. eldest daughter of MR. WILLIAM O. BANNON, all of Wilkinson county.

Died – On Saturday, the 28th ult., a half past 5o'clock, P.M. Col. STEPHEN SWAIN, of Decatur county, aged 80 years two months and eighteen days. The deceased was an affectionate husband, a tender parent and kind master...The day before his death, he expressed a willingness to die...He passed off in a pleasant sleep, without a struggle or a groan.

In Laurens county, at half-past 12 o'clock, A.M. on Monday, the 1st inst., after an illness of eight days, MRS. FANNIE N. KELLUM, wife of MR. G. T. KELLUM, and daughter of the late SAM'L BUFFINGTON, of Milledgeville, aged 20 years and three days.

On Sunday morning, March 7th, of congestion of the brain, after an illness of three days, CONWAY FORTESCUE only son of MR. and MRS. L. N. WHITTLE, aged 4 years, 5 months and 23 days.

In this city, on Wednesday night last, JOHN HENRY MORGAN, aged about 38 years. He was buried with Masonic honors on Thursday.

In this city, on Tuesday evening last, MR. MIDAS L. GRAYBILL, aged 42 years, after a lingering illness of many months. On Thursday morning his remains were interred according to Masonic ceremonies.

On Thursday last MRS. SARAH A. USHER, a highly respectable widow lady of this city, aged 74 years.

Issue of March 23, 1852

Death of Col. WM. S. KING – It becomes our painful duty to announce the death of Col. W. S. KING, one of the proprietors of the Charleston Courier, who departed this life yesterday, in the 51st year of his age, at his residence in this city, between the hours of one and two o'clock P.M.

Married – On the 11th inst., by the Rev. G. H. CLIETT, MR. ABSALOM AMAKER, of Richmond county, to MISS ABBEY ANN BASTON, of Columbia county.

On the 26th ult., at St. Peter's Church, Baltimore Md., by Rev. THOMAS ATKINSON, D.D. Col. WM. N. NELSON, of Columbus, Ga., to MISS MARY A. PAGE, youngest daughter of the late WM. BYRD POAGE, of Page Brook, Clarke county, Va.

On the 7th inst., by the Rev. T. J. THRELKELD, MR. WILLIAM C. HUDSON, to MISS FRANCIS WILLIS, all of the city of Oglethorpe.

On the same morning, at the residence of WM. WILDER, Esq. by the Rev. P. L. J. MAY, O. J. REGISTER, Esq. to MISS TOMESIA SHERMAN, all of that place.

In Marion county, on Tuesday the 8th inst., by Rev. P. L. J. MAY, MR. WM. W. HILL, of Oglethorpe, to MISS ELIZABETH MILLER, of Macon county.

Died – In Columbus, on the 4th inst., MRS. SARAH VIVIAN, daughter of Major J. H. HOWARD, and wife of MR. JAMES W. WARREN, of that city.

At the residence of MR. WILLIAM BROOKS, in Columbus, on the 11th inst., GEORGE C. HODGES, Esq. of Barbour co., Ala., aged 56 years.

Issue of March 30, 1852

Died – At his residence near Newnan, on Tuesday 23d inst., after a long and painful illness, GILBERT D. GREER, Esq. in about the 60th year of his age.

At his residence in Newnan, on the 22d inst., WILLIAM NIMMONS, Esq. aged 53 years.

Issue of April 13, 1852

Marriage – In this city, on the 4th inst., by the Rev. SAMUEL ANTHONY, MR. THOMAS SHINHOLSTER to MISS MALINDA M. daughter of WILLIAM B. GAMBLE, Esq. of this city.

On the 30th ult., in Houston county, by the Rev. B. F. THARP, Rev. S. LANDRUM, Pastor of the Baptist church, in this city to MISS ELIZA JANE WARREN, daughter of Gen. ELI WARREN.

Died – At the residence of GEORGE BENTON, in Troup co., on the 27th ult., A. M. WILKINSON, M. S. in the 25th year of his age.

In LaGrange, on the evening of the 27th ult., in the 20th year of her age, MRS. MARY HAWKINS MORGAN; wife of MR. ROBERT J. MORGAN, and daughter of the late DR. ANDREW and MRS. CAROLINE M. BATTLE.

Issue of April 20, 1852

RUFUS GREENE, of Mobile, charged with forging the name of DANIEL ROBERTSON, to a bond of $25,000, to the Farmer's Insurance Company, of which GREENE was Secretary, has been convicted, and sentenced to ten years Imprisonment, in the Penitentiary of Alabama.

Died – At his residence, near Hawkinsville, on the 30th ult., DR. WILLIAM MARTIN FRASER, aged 34 years.

Issue of April 27, 1852

Death of Marshal RADETSESKY – Rumored Death of CHARLES KEAN – Boston April 17 – Letters received by the America, from Turin, mention the death of Marshal RADETSESKY. The sudden death of CHARLES KEAN, while performing upon the stage, is also reported.
Second Dispatch – A letter to MR. DICKINSON the tragedian, states that MR. KEAN, was taken alarmingly ill on the night of the 1st April, while playing King John, at the Prince's Theatre, London. Permission was asked of the Queen, who was present, to stop the play – to which she gave her consent, and another piece was substituted.

Death of Judge MERIWETHER – It is with painful regret, we announce, the death of Judge MERIWETHER. He died at his residence on Saturday last, of Typhoid Pneumonia, having been confined by that disease about a week.

Married – On the 15th inst., by the Rev. J. RUFUS FELDER, MR. JOHN H. KING, to MISS F. CAMILLA KILLEN, both of Perry, Houston county, Georgia.

In Irwin county, by JAMES SMITH, Esq. Col. CLARK WILLCOX, of Telfair county, to MISS JANE E., youngest daughter of SMAUEL FULLER, Esq. of Irwin county.

Died – At Washington City, on the 14th inst., CHARLES HENRY BAILEY, infant son of the Hon. D. J. BAILEY, of Georgia, aged about two years.

Issue of May 4, 1852

Death from Chloroform – MRS. EMILY NORTON, wife of H. Z. NORTON, of Norwalk, Conn., died at New Haven, on

Friday from chloroform, taken to aid the extraction of teeth. It appears she was afflicted with a disease of the jaw, requiring the extraction of several diseased teeth. She had last year taken chloroform with happy effect and on this occasion, intending to have a tooth drawn, insisted on DR. PARK, her medical attendant, again administering it. The Journal says: "She was allowed to inhale the chloroform in very small quantities for several minutes; and almost while she was saying she felt no effect from it, and was asking for its free administration, the doctor noticed the pulse suddenly to fall. Within three or four minutes from the time this change was noticed all signs of life were gone, and the most vigorous efforts to resusitate the woman proved unavailing. An inquest was held over her remains, and, on the testimony of several physicians, DR.PARK was exculpated from all blame. One half a drachm of chloroform, which was inhaled from a sponge, was used.

Death of Professor EDWARDS – The religious public as well as scholars generally throughout the country, will hear with deep regret of the death of this excellent man and thorough scholar, which took place during the past week at Athens, Ga., where he had spent the winter in the hope of regaining his health. DR. EDWARDS was Associate Professor of Sacred Literature in the Theological Seminary at Andover, where for a _____ of year he had done good service in upholding, and even advancing, the reputation of an institution...His remains passed through this city on Saturday, accompanied by his afflicted family and brother, Col. EDWARDS, of Southhampton.

Marriage at a Fancy Ball – The New York Herald, says: A fancy ball was given at Syracuse on the evening of the 8th inst., when, among other incidents of the evening, was the marriage by Justice JOHNSON of MR. JAMES DORAN, who appeared in the brilliant costume of a knight of Malta, in which he appeared to good advantage, to MISS

BARTLETT, a dark eyed beauty, who was elegantly attired in the dress of a Greek girl. The audience was requested to preserve order for a few moments, and, to the surprise of most of those present, the young, handsome, and elegantly attired bride and bridegroom stepped to the middle of the floor, and the marriage ceremony was performed in the midst of a gay and brilliant assembly of representatives from every quarter of the globe. After the justice had pronounced them 'husband and wife', he retired from the room, and the dance went on 'merrily as the marriage bells'.

Death of Prince SCHWARZENBERG. The London Times announces the sudden decease, by apoplexy, of Prince SCHWARZENBERG, the celebrated Austrian Prime Minister, which occurred at Vienna on the 5th of April. He was the most eminent man in the empire...He was the leader of the reactionary movement that commenced in 1848, and it is to his counsels, backed as they were by Russia, that the defeat of Hungary is to be attributed. His death will prove a terrible blow to the House of Hapsburg.

Married – On the 15th inst., in Twiggs county, by the Rev. DAVID ROBERTS, Rev. JAS. W. TRAWICK, of the Georgia Conference, to MISS PENELOPE A. BROWN, of Twiggs county.

Near Sandersville, on the 22d inst., by the Rev. JAS. R. SMITH, MR. W. ABNEY to MISS GRACY BAILEY.

71

$5 Reward – Ranaway from (near CARLETON'S steam mill) South Western Railroad by boy JOHN, aged about 40 years, very black, about 5 feet 7 inches high, speaks slow. The above reward will be paid for him if arrested in Bibb county, and a reasonable reward if apprehended out of the county, and he is returned to me, or lodged in Bibb county Jail.

JAS T. HUMPHRIES
Per GEO. W. ADAMS, Sup't. S.W.R.R.

<u>Issue of May 11, 1852</u>

Prize Fight – One of these brutal exhibitions came off in the vicinity of New York on Tuesday, between two men named CLARE and LEES. CLARE was victorious. LEES at the end of the seventh round received a severe blow, which it was thought had killed him, when the whole party of seconds and spectators took to flight. CLARE jumped from the ring and ran with the crowd, outstripping in speed the best man. LEES, however, recovered in short time afterwards, and was accompanied by his friends to their boat.

Death of JOHN MCLEAN, Esq. We clip the following notice of the demise of a gentleman well known in our community from the Cherow Gazette: "We regret to learn from a letter received by a gentleman of this place, that JOHN MCLEAN, Esq. for many years a large mail contractor in this State, died at his residence, Scotch Grove, near Laurel Hill, Richmond county, N. C. on the 24th inst. He was in the prime of life, though for some time in feeble health. He leaves an extended circle of friends and relations to mourn his early death."

Married – In Newnan, Thursday evening, the 29th ult., by Rev. ROBERT FLEMING, FR. A. R. WELLBORN to MISS

GEORGE A. RAY, eldest daughter of JOHN RAY, Esq., and all of Newnan.

On the 29th ult., by Rev. A. W. OGILVIE, M. RICHARD W. FARRELL, of Ireland, to MISS MARY KERSEY of Coweta county.

On Sunday morning, the 2d inst., by the same, DR. JAMES R. THOMASSON, of Bowenville, Carroll county, Ga., to MISS MARIA L. COLBERT, daughter of Rev. THOS. COLBERT of Coweta.

Died – In this city on Wednesday night last, Maj. JAMES SMITH, an old and highly respectable citizen.

In Telfair on the 6th ult., General MARK WILCOX, after a short but severe illness.

Issue of May 18, 1852

Drowned – In Flint river, near Bainbridge, Ga., on the 6th inst., BENJAMIN RUFUS, youngest son of the late RUFUS K. EVANS of this city, aged about 12 years. The body was found on the 10(?)th inst.

Outrage at Richmond – The capitol of Virginia was the scene, a few days ago, of a most lawless, ferocious and disgraceful popular outbreak. On the evening of the 7th inst., a large crowd congregated around the Executive Mansion, at Richmond, and offered various demonstrations of disrespect and insult to the Governor of that State, in consequence of his having commuted the punishment of a negro who had been sentenced to be hung, for murdering a white man. The legislature has appointed a committee to enquire into the facts concerning this most disgraceful affair.

Swallowing a Chinquepin – We find the following letter in the Milledgeville Recorder, dated Lowndes co., Ga., the 2d inst. Gentlemen: I wish to give you the particulars of a strange circumstance which has taken place in this neighborhood a few days since. In the year 1845, a little boy the son of MR. ASHLEY LAWSON, got strangled in trying to swallow a chinquepin, and from that time he has been troubled with a cough similar to croupe every winter. This spring his parents thought he would die, (being worse off than usual) but he coughed up the chinquepin. On examination it had a bony covering about one sixteenth of an inch thick on it. On removing the osseous substance, the chinquepin was found to be perfectly sound, the marks were on it where he had scraped it with his knife before trying to swallow it. He is now in good health and free from the cough, with which he has been troubled so long. In conclusion, I would say, that there are many respectable persons who will vouch for the truth of the above statement.

JAS. R. FOLSOM

Death of Distinguished Persons – Miss AMELIA B. WELBY, the poetess, and Col. W. B. JONES, of the United States Army, died at Louisville on Monday the 3d inst.

Married – In this city, on the 11th inst., by the Rev. S. LANDRUM, MR. JOHN W. CRUMP, to MISS FRANCIS WATTERS.

In this city, on the 12th inst., by Rev. S. LANDRUM, MR. JOHN HOLTZENDORF, to MISS ELIZA CASSEDY.

In Christ church in this city on Wednesday evening, the 12th inst., by the Rev. J. A. SHANKLIN, MR. JOHN S. HUTTON, to MISS HARRIET, daughter of NATHAN C. MONROE, Esq. of Vineville.

In Milledgeville, on Thursday evening, the 6th inst., by the Rev. MR. HINTON, MR. JOHN W. W. SNEAD, to MISS MARY A., eldest daughter of the late Rev. JOHN B. DAVIES, and granddaughter of the late Judge DAVIES, of Savannah.

On the 27th of April, by the Rev. JOHN P. DICKINSON, MR. KINCHEN P. THWEATT, to MISS EUPHEMIA L. daughter of the Rev. THOMAS FLEWELLEN, all of Upson county.

In Charleston, on Thursday evening, 6th inst., by the Rev. DR. HANCKEL, CHARLES A. A. DUNWOODY, Esq. of Roswell, Ga., to MISS ELLEN C., only daughter of the Hon. WM. RICE, of Charleston, S. C.

Died – In this city, on Monday the 10th inst., MRS. ANN MCGOWN, a native of the county of Cavan, Ireland, but for many years a resident of this place, aged 58 years.

Issue of May 25, 1852

Death of MRS. ADAMS – MRS. ADAMS, the venerable relict of the late JOHN QUINCY ADAMS, Ex-President of the United States, died at her residence on F Street in Washington City, on Saturday the 15th inst.

Died – Suddenly on the 26th inst., in Monroe co., Geo., WARREN BARROW, Esq. aged 69 years. He was born in Beaufort county, North Carolina, and removed to Georgia at the age of nineteen years. He resided many years in Warren, Hancock, and Putnam, and for the last 22 years in Monroe county. He was for upwards of 24 years a worthy and acceptable member of the Baptist church and at the time of his death a much beloved deacon in that church. The deceased through life sustained the character of an honest, reliable man, the noblest work of God.

Departed this life on the morning of the 18th inst., at the house of Maj. JOHN F. SPICER, where she had gone on a visit, after a long illness, MRS. SARAH ELIZA PACE, consort of DAVIS PACE, Esq. of Albany, Ga., in the 26th year of her age. She leaves a large circle of friends and relatives, a devoted husband and two little children to deplore her loss.

Issue of June 1, 1852

Unfortunate Affair between two relatives – Hon. EDWARD A. HANNEGAN, late U. S. Senator from Indiana, and Capt. DUNCAN, his brother-in-law, living in the same house at Covington, Indiana, on the most friendly terms, had a personal misunderstanding on the 7th ult. It appears that on the day and evening previous, they had both been drinking, and that on the morning of the sad occurrence, Capt. DUNCAN went upstairs to MR. HANNEGAN'S room, and an altercation ensued between the parties, when Capt. DUNCAN gave MR. HANNEGAN a slap in the face. MR. HANNEGAN, upon the indignity he felt, and the impulse of the moment, struck Capt. DUNCAN with a knife in the lower part of the stomach, inflicting a severe and what is thought, a dangerous wound. MR. HANNEGAN recovering from his passions, aroused by the supposed indignity, suffers the most excruciating tortures in the reflection that he has, perhaps, struck down as kind a friend as he has on earth. The Lafayette (Ohio) Journal says: "To all inquiries as to the cause of the difficulties, its origin, etc. Capt. DUNCAN invariably replied, "Nothing, it was nothing!" and seemed determined not to reveal anything that would afford additional evidence against MR. HANNEGAN. It is said that a short time before he died, he observed that he himself was to blame. It is thought by some that he made private declarations as to the whole matter, but if so, they have not yet been made public. He died after suffering the most intense pain, calm and composed, at 12 o'clock on Saturday, fully and freely

forgiving MR. HANNEGAN.   Immediately after the
occurrence, Capt. DUNCAN requested the Masonic
fraternity, of which both he and MR. HANNEGAN were
members, to take him in charge. They did so, and he was
buried with the honors of that order on Sunday afternoon.
The funeral took place from MR. HANNEGAN'S residence,
where Capt. DUNCAN died. The latter was the only living
brother of MRS. HANNEGAN, who still lives, the object of
universal pity. The anguish of MR. HANNEGAN'S mind is
said to be intense and excruciating. The consequences of
his rash act have driven him to a state bordering on
despair.

Captain DUNCAN raised a troop of horse in Licking
county, Ohio, during the Mexican War, and served
gallantly on the field of battle. He was brave, noble and
generous, and as a merchant in Covington for the last two
years, was highly esteemed for his gentlemanly demeanor.
MR. HANNEGAN and himself had always been warm
friends, but, unfortunately, they were both intemperate,
and at the time of the occurrence, as well as the day
previous, were intoxicated with liquor.

Married – At Chunnynuggee, Ala., on Tuesday, the 11th
ult., by the Rev. SAMUEL HENDERSON, MR. EDWARD
J. WHITE to MISS_____COTTON.

Died – At Pilatka, Fla., on the 11th ult., KATE WISE infant
daughter of JOS B. and SARAH J. ASKEW, aged two
months and six days.

...announcing the sudden demise of MR. M. C. MURPHEY,
a citizen of Atlanta, and an officer on the Georgia Road.
His death was caused by a relapse of measles, which
hurried him to the grave in a very few days. He was
perfectly conscious until within a few hours of his death
and on the morning of the 21st inst. his weary spirit took its
flight...

Issue of June 8, 1852

Married – In this city on the 2d inst., by Rev. S. LANDRUM, MR. LEWIS B. WOOD, to MISS MARTHA A. OLIVER.

Issue of June 15, 1852

Death of Rev. DR. NOTT – The venerable DR. SAMUEL NOTT died at his residence, in Franklin Conn., on the 26th ult., in the 99th year of his age. About a week before his death his gown caught fire, while sitting alone in his room, and before it was extinguished his hand was badly burned. The injury. The injury and excitement consequent upon the accident, probably hastened his death. DR. NOTT had been settled in the parish more than seventy years, and was probably the oldest pastor of a parish in New England, or perhaps in the United States. He officiated in the pulpit until he reached the age of 94 years. His funeral was attended by an immense concourse of people, embracing those within a circle of twenty miles in diameter.

Married – In Bibb county, on Tuesday the 8th inst., by Rev. E. H. MYERS, President of the Wesleyan Female College, DR. JOHN CALDERWOOD, of Monroe, La., to MISS LOUISA HUNTER, daughter of Col. SAMUEL B. HUNTER.

In Pike county, on the 10th inst., by the Rev. JOHN P. DICKINSON, MR. GEORGE W. FACELER, of Upson county to MISS MARTHA WILLIAMS, of Pike county.

Obituary – Departed this life, on the morning of the 22d ult., in Monroe county, MRS. EVALINE A. CHAPMAN, wife of AMBROSE CHAPMAN, Esq. and daughter of JOHN FREEMAN, Esq., aged 33 years.

Tribute of Respect – JOHN HARTWELL TARVER

Issue of June 22, 1852

Married – In Crawford county, on the 17th inst., by WILLIAM L. HUNT, Esq., MR. JAMES G. BROWN, of Dooly county, to MISS SARAH ELIZA, eldest daughter of MATHEW J. and SARAH JORDAN, of Crawford county.

Died – On the 25 May, aged about 27 years, MRS. AMANDA M. BANKS, wife of JOSEPH R. BANKS, of Pike and daughter of A. and N. DAVIS of Monroe county, Ga.

Issue of June 29, 1852

Died – In East Macon, on the 27th inst., MR. LESLIE L. COATES, aged 25 years.

Married – In Marietta, Ga., on the 15th inst., by B. TOLLESON, Ordinary of Cobb county, MR. GEORGE WASHINGTON FLOURNOY to MISS EMILY CAROLINE GRIFFIES.

At the residence of Col. WIGGINS, in Waynesville, on the 31st ult., by the Rev. H. K. REES, DR. A. WALTHOUR, of Liberty county to MISS CALLIE A. daughter of WM. M. MORTON, Esq. of Athens, Ga.

In Jackson county, Ga., on the 17th inst. by Elder D. W. PATMAN, MR. ORIEN T. TARRY, of Lincolnton, Ga., (formerly of New York) to MISS NANCY PATMAN of the former place.

On the 9th inst., by Rev. JAMES H. GEORGE, MR. THOMAS F. HAMPTON, of Albany, to MISS ELIZA, daughter of JOSHUA B. OLIVER, Esq. of Baker county, Ga.

In Washington county, on the 15th inst., by Rev. MR. SHANKLIN, MR. O. H. PRINCE, of Macon, to MISS

SARAH M. R. JACKSON, daughter of the late DR. HENRY JACKSON, of Athens, Ga.

Issue of July 6, 1852

Death of HENRY CLAY

Issue of July 20, 1852

Married – In Crawford county, on the 8th inst., by JOHN F. TAYLOR, Esq. JAMES D. HARTLY, Esq. to MISS EPSEY THAMES, all of Crawford county.

Died – In Thomaston, on the 10th instant, MRS. ANN MOORE. In her death there was lost a kind neighbor and Christian, a devoted wife and affectionate mother.

Died of Congestive Fever, on Saturday, June 26th, at her residence in Crawford county, MRS. NANCY CLEVELAND, consort of the Rev. W. C. CLEVELAND, aged 49 years 3 months and 29 days. MRS. CLEVELAND had been a member of the Baptist church for 24 years.

Brutal Murder of a School Girl – MISS MARY ANN BELL, a girl of sixteen summers, left her mother's residence in Monroe county, Miss., to go to school, a mile distant, and not returning at sunset, her mother became alarmed, and had her hunter. The near neighbors assisted in the search, mounted on horses, with torches, and the corpse was found about two or three o'clock, next morning, in a path leading from the school house towards home, her eyes and mouth closed, lying on her face, all her clothes in a proper manner, her bonnet on and no sign of blood. Upon examination, marks of strangulation were found about her neck, various bruises upon her body, and evident sign of her having been violated by some inhuman fiend. A meeting of the citizens was at once called, and the most searching investigation instituted, but without avail.

A veteran – There is at present residing in the town of Bertre, Canada, a few miles below Waterloo, a man named SILAS CASTER, who was formerly a coachman in the employ of Gen. WASHINGTON. His age is 96 years, and he is in the perfect enjoyment of his health and all his faculties. He settled in Canada in the year of 1800, and has been residing there ever since, and occasionally visits Buffalo.

Issue of July 27, 1852

The Murder of Bv't Lt. Col. CRAIG of the Army. The Washington Union publishes letters of this gallant and lamented officer, who was murdered near San Diego, California, by Corporal HAYS and Private CONDON of D Company, Indiana Infantry. "The circumstances of his death illustrate the character of the man, and are briefly these: Colonel CRAIG, on the morning of the 6th inst., when about one third of the way across the desert from this side, met two deserters from Camp Yuma, trying to make their way into the settlements. They were on foot, and armed with percussion muskets. The Colonel and his party were on mules. He pursued the deserters, taking with him two sergeants, who, like himself, were armed with pistols and sabers. He followed them two or three miles, urging them to surrender, and stating to them that he did not intend to use force. At length, the deserters halted, and Colonel CRAIG, taking off his sabre and pistols, and handing them to a sergeant in their presence, dismounted, and unarmed approached them, addressing them at the same time. The Colonel's mule having strayed at that moment, one of the sergeants went to catch it. In the act of doing so, he heard two shots in rapid succession. Turning his head he saw the Colonel and Sergeant BEALS fall. They then commenced firing on him, when he put spur to his horse and fled to camp. A party was immediately sent out. The body of Col. CRAIG was found, and near it the sergeant, who had been wounded in the leg, the same ball killing his mule. The wounded sergeant stated that Colonel CRAIG was fired upon when within a few feet of the deserters; received the shot in the front and lower part of his body; did not speak, and expired in about ten minutes. He was buried in the desert, at a place called the "Alamo Wells!"

The murderers were arrested by the Indians at Tamacala, and will surely meet their reward, for at the last accounts the sergeant was recovering to supply any link wanting in the chain of events.

Col. CRAIG is well known in this State, and married one of the most amiable and beautiful daughters of the Rev. DR. CHURCH, President of the State University at Athens. At the time of his death, he was in command of the military escort of the boundary commission.

Died – On the 20th July, 1852, in Jefferson county, Georgia, DR. JOSEPH SAGE, of inflammation of the bowels, aged thirty years. DR. SAGE was a native of Perth, Scotland, from whence he emigrated in 1845, since which time he has been a resident and citizen of Georgia. He was a most efficient member of the profession...

In Monroe county, on the 19th inst., MARY ANN, daughter of EDMUND S. and AMELIA CHAMBLISS, in the 10th year of her age.

Twenty-five Dollars Reward, will be paid for the confinement of my negro man CAIN in the Jail at Macon, Bibb county. CAIN is well known in the vicinity of Jeffersonville, Twiggs county, and in the city of Macon.

Issue of August 3, 1852

Bodies Recovered from the Wreck of the Steamer Henry Clay – Georgians Aboard. Twenty three bodies have been recovered from the wreck of the steamer Henry Clay, burnt yesterday; on the Hudson river. Fifty or sixty passengers are still missing, among them MR. and MRS. FENNELL, of Wilmington, North Carolina, the wife and two children of Prof. BAILEY, of West Point, (well known in Savannah,) and ex-Mayor ALLEN of New York. MISS TUCKER, of Milledgeville, Ga., was seriously burned; also, WILLIS B. PRESCOTT, of Louisiana. Baggage marked M. A. F. , MISS H. CLEMENS, and L. E. B., Wilmington, (N. C.) has been recovered, for which no owners have been found. The fire was caused by the excessive heat while racing the steamer North America. At the time – four o'clock in the morning – nearly all the passengers were in their berths. The scene is described as heart-rending and terrible.

Massacre of U. S. Troops – Captain MARCY and Eighty Men Killed. Our New Orleans exchanges received yesterday contain news, brought by an express from Fort Arbuckle, the outer frontier station, of the murder of Capt. MARCY and his command of 80 men, by the Commanches. Capt. MARCY was on an exploring expedition to the head waters of Red river. The Commanches in number about 2,000, first stampeded the horses and mules in the night, and attacked the troops, and fought them during the whole of the next day before they succeeded in killing all. It is believed by the officers at Fort Smith, that all the wild tribes are concentrating for a general assault on the posts and settlements, and that an Indian war is inevitable. The government has, on that frontier, only one-half a regiment.

A Windfall – A young lady of Brooklyn, named PAYNE, ahs recently received a legacy amounting to 75,000 pounds from a DON GUY EMANUEL HERNANDO, a wealthy West India planter. This lady, it is said, was married to the planter in 1846, when she was scarcely 15 years old, but the marriage having proved an unhappy one, it was never proclaimed. Shortly after, he left her and took up his residence in New Orleans. In 1848 he received information of his father's death – he returned to his estate in South America, and succeeded in increasing his already large fortune to 150,000 pounds. As he was about to embark for Havanna, he was taken with the cholera, and died on his estate, bequeathing 75,000 pounds to his wife, (if living), and the whole if she never married and resided on his estate, which will render her the wealthiest heiress in the United States.

N. Y. Post

Married – On the 20th ult. by the Rev. DR. DOUGLAS, MR. WM. E. WILSON, of Atlanta, and MISS SUSANNA E. WARD, daughter of Rev. JAMES WARD, of Burke county, Ga.

On the 26th ult. by the Rev. JONES E. SHARP, MR. JOHN M. SHARP, of Monroe, to MISS MARTHA W. SANDERS, of Bibb county.

Death of GEORGE GLENN, Esq. We regret to record the rather sudden and unexpected death of our worthy fellow citizen, GEORGE GLENN, Esq. He expired at his residence yesterday, about 1 (?) o'clock P. M. The deceased was a native of the city of Savannah, and has long been known as the efficient Clerk of the District Court of the United States for the Southern District of Georgia, which office he has held for about the last thirty years...MR. GLENN had, at least, attained the Scriptural age allotted to man. He was never married, but has left a large circle of relatives, friends, and acquaintances, to mourn his decease... His funeral will take place this afternoon at 5 o'clock.

Issue of August 10, 1852

Judge DEVAUX, a wealthy resident of Baltimore, died at Niagara on Wednesday.

Capt. MARCY – The Little Rock Gazette of July 30, has a statement from Fort Arbuckle that the reported massacre of Capt. MARCY and his corps, is a hoax.

Died – At the Indian Springs, on the 5th inst. CLARENCE WESTON, only child of DR. ROBERT M. and MRS. JULIA E. PETTERSON, aged 15 months.

Funeral Notice – The friends and acquaintances of Gen. H. MCLEOD and family are requested to attend the funeral of his child, from the residence of ALEXANDER MELROSE, Esq., in East Macon, at 1 o'clock this afternoon, without further notice.

Fifty Dollars Reward – Ranaway from the subscriber on the 25th day of December last, a negro man named HENRY, about thirty years old, of dark complexion; six feet high and weighs about 180 lbs, with a slight scar over one eye, and a small scar on one arm below the elbow. I bought the negro from FRILY J. HARRISON, of Randolph county, Ga., who brought him from Jasper county. I will give the above reward, if delivered to me in Randolph county, or in any safe jail in the State, so that I get him. Also, I will give $200 if harbored by any white man, with proof sufficient to convict him.

ROBT S. HATCHER

Issue of August 17, 1852

Safety of Capt. MARCY and his command. We received yesterday, says the New Orleans Crescent, of the 9th inst., Little Rock papers, containing intelligence from Fort Smith, that Capt. MARCY and his command were safe.

Died – In Barnesville, August 6th, from typhoid fever, aged 26 years and 10 months, EMILY C., wife of C. A.

NUTTING, and daughter of JORDAN COMPTON, Esq., of Jasper county, Ga.

In this city on the 11th inst., MR. THOMAS F. NEWTON, a native of the State of Maryland but for the last sixteen years a resident of this city.

Issue of August 24, 1852

Married – In this county, on the morning of the 17th inst., by STERLING TUCKER, Esq., Col. JAMES D. VAN VALKENBURG, to MISS MARY E. K. MORGAN of Monroe county.

At the residence of Maj. HENRY CLARK, on the 18th inst., by the Rev. SAMUEL ANTHONY, MR. WM. B. HEATH to MISS EFFIE C. RILEY, all of this city.

Died – In this city, on Friday morning, 20th inst., SABINA, only daughter of FRANCIS S. and DOLORES B. HERNANDEZ, aged one year and twenty days.

Issue of August 31, 1852

Death by Accident – It is with pain we record the death at a few minutes past 3 o'clock, yesterday afternoon, of MR. COFFEE, first engineer of the steam ship State of Georgia. The steamer was to have sailed at half past three for Philadelphia, and he was engaged in the engine room, as is customary, in getting the machinery in working order. The engine had been put in motion, and was working slowly when the cross head descending, caught MR. COFFEE between it and the cylinder head. He was found with his face downward, and some of the cylinder head had been forced into his chest. It is supposed he had reached forward to oil or adjust something while the piston was ascending, and that he did not withdraw in ____ when the engine returned to its lower center. Medical attendance was immediately obtained, but the injuries received were so severe, that he died in twenty minutes. We learn that MR. COFFEE was much esteemed as an engineer and an honorable and upright man. He has acted in the capacity of first engineer of the State of Georgia since she commenced running. He was a native of Philadelphia, where his family reside, consisting of a wife and three children. The steamer sailed at 4 o'clock, after having been supplied with an engineer from the steamship Alabama. Her colors were displayed at half mast as she passed out. The body remains on board, and will be taken to Philadelphia for interment.

Melancholy Suicide – Quite a painful sensation was produced in our community yesterday afternoon, by the startling report that a young physician by the name of JOSEPH M. BOGGS, had committed suicide in his room at MRS. PLATT'S Boarding House on Pulaski Square. He was first discovered between three and four o'clock in the afternoon, lying on the floor of his sleeping room by his office boy, who immediately gave the alarm DR. BIRD being sent for was among the first who entered the room, where he found the deceased lying in a very composed attitude on his back, his head resting upon a pillow which he had place on the back of a chair turned down for the purpose. On the floor, by his side, were a tumbler and an empty phial which had contained prussic acid and to his breast, over which his hands were studiously composed, was the following note, written in a free bold hand: "I have taken half an ounce of Prussic Acid. You can prove it by going to Lincoln's or formerly Turner and Co's.

JOS. M. BOGGS

August 24, 1852, half past one o'clock. The verdict of the Coroner's inquest was in accordance with the above facts. DR. BOGGS was, we believe, a native of South Carolina, and had resided in this city several years.

87

Death of DR. MCWHORTER. It is our painful task to record the death of DR. J. G. MCWHORTER, who, for many years, has been a highly respected and prominent citizen of this community, and has long been well known and esteemed throughout the State. After retiring from professional practice, he was, for a few years, editor and proprietor of a leading journal in this city, and until recent years, to take a warm interest in public affairs. His health had been feeble and declining for some time, and his death is the close of a tedious and distressing illness. He was a gentleman of upright and honorable deportment.

Married – In Bibb county, on Thursday evening 26th inst., by SOLMON R. JOHNSON, Esq., MR. HENRY G. ROSS, JR. to MISS FRANCES O. GORMAN, daughter of DR. THOMAS B. GORMAN, all of Macon.

Issue of September 7, 1852

Obituary – JOSEPH ADKINS, died at his residence in Wilkinson county, near Irwinton, on the 29th ult. He has left a bereaved and disconsolate family to mourn his loss.

Died – In Barnesville, on the 1st inst., (of derangement of the brain) WILEY BRANTLEY, infant son of J. P. & MARY E. MOYE, aged three weeks and four days.

Suicide with a Moral – A man by the name of JOHN S. DAVIS, of West Jersey Ferry opposite Philadelphia, committed suicide a short time since under very singular circumstances (long article).

A Student Drowned – We regret to learn that a young student attached to the Georgia University at Athens, by the name of FRANCIS BRYAN, whose parents reside in Jackson county, Florida, lost his life on the 30th, in attempting to cross the river near Athens. He was in a small canoe, which got entangled in some drift wood, which caused it to upset, and he was drowned before any assistance could reach him.

Another Revolutionary Soldier Gone – JAMES WOOL, another of the heroes of the Revolution died on Wednesday, near, Troy, on the farm where his father lived and died. In 1776, the family was impelled to flee from their home and seek safety for their women and children. This done, the men___ ___to battle, and never laid down their arms____victory had crowned them. JEREMIAH WOOL was_____the Committee of Safety for the City of New_____. ISAIAH WOOL was a captain in LAMB'S regi_____Artillery; he went with MONTGOMERY to Quebec and was afterwards severely wounded in New_____ near Washington. ROBERT and ELLIS WOOL_____taken prisoners at Fort Washington, and lodged_____Jersey prison ship, where ELLIS died. JOHN WOOL, the father of Gen. JOHN E. WOOL, was with_____at the storming of Stony Point. JAMES, the _____of the present notice, was the youngest of the_____. "I was a tall, strong boy," said he, "and they____fight at Bennington." He was fifteen then. _____of more than eighty winters had___his locks and palsied limbs, he loved to_____there scenes and thank God that he had permitted him to see his children's children_____the blessings he had helped to win.

Issue of September 14, 1852

Death of Georgians in California – The Augusta Constitutionalist says: Among the deaths in Sacramento Valley, we notice the following: Died suddenly on the 22dJuly, at Hawkins bar, Toulomne river, Col. THOMAS MYERS, late of Macon county, Ga. Among the interments at San Francisco, we notice the name of MR. L. D. BUEL, of Georgia, aged 30 years, buried July 11th, and the name of JESSE WALTHINGHAM, of Georgia, aged 38 years, buried July 13th.

89

Mysterious Disappearance – We understand that a passenger from New York on the Alabama, has not been seen or heard of since early on Tuesday morning last. When the vessel arrived in port and the passengers were departing, he was not present to claim his truck, which is still in the possession of the Agents. He entered his name as H. N. PAGE of Macon, Ga. The trunk is of brown leather and medium size. It is feared that he may have been lost overboard. Papers in the city might perhaps confer a favor on the relatives of the deceased, by publishing this paragraph. Savannah Courier, 11th inst.

Duel in New Jersey- The New York Sun gives an account of a duel which was fought on Wednesday, in New Jersey, by Capt. STONE of Santa Fe, and MR. TOWNLY, of New Bedford. The alleged cause of the quarrel was some insult offered by MR. TOWNLY to a cousin of Capt. STONE, who demanded an apology on Tuesday evening, at a Theatre in Broadway, which being refused, the Captain knocked MR. TOWNLY down. Thereupon, MR. TOWNLY sent his "friend" MR. GROOME, with a challenge, which was accepted, and in pursuance of which the duel was fought. The name of the Captain's second is said to be STANTON. Three shots were exchanged, and MR. TOWNLY was wounded in the hip and shoulder, while the Captain escaped with a bullet hole through his hat. A surgeon, who accompanied the parties, dressed the wounds, and the duelists and "friends" returned to the city.

A Sad Story – MISS IDA WILLIAMS, a beautiful and talented young English lady, twenty-three years of age, who was rescued from the steamboat Atlantic, has arrived at Detroit. The Advertiser, of that city says: "She had just arrived in this country from England, and was traveling westward with a view to select a location for a future residence, in company with a twin brother, a married sister, a brother-in-law, and two nieces, all of whom were

90

lost. She states that the last recollection she has of anything which took place on the Atlantic, she was standing in company with her friends on the deck, when a beam or piece of wood fell and killed her brother and hitting her also in its fall, injured her back when she fainted. She had no consciousness of anything which took place afterwards, until she found herself on board the propeller on her way to Erie, without clothing, except her night dress, without money, and without a friend on this side of the broad Atlantic – her friends were all lost! Without knowing where to turn for succor, she took passage on a Detroit boat and reached this city, where her immediate wants were supplied, and where she had been kindly offered a home in the family of a highly respectable and hospitable resident of Detroit."

Married – In Lee county, on the 2d inst. by the Rev. MR. DAVIS, Col. RICHARD H. CLARK and MISS ANNIE M. LOTT.

In Penfield, Ga., on the 24th ult. by the Rev. N. M. CRAWFORD, MR. R. H. SAPP, Esq. of Burke county, to MISS SARAH M. KELLAM of the former place.

Died – At his residence in Macon county, on the 9th inst. MR. URIAH SLAPPEY, aged fifty-four years.

Issue of September 21, 1852

Suicide – Surgeon D. C. MCLEOD, at the U. S. Naval Hospital, Pensacola, committed suicide on the 1st inst., by cutting his throat with a razor. He was buried with military honors.

Married – In Crawford county, Ga., on the 19th ult., at the house of DAVID BOWERS, by C.H. WALKER, Esq., MR. JAMES C. ROBERSON to SARAH CATHERINE BOWERS.

Died – On Saturday morning, 10th inst., at the house of his father-in-law, PETER ARNOLD, in the city of Macon, Georgia, MR. WILLIAM ALBERT SIMS, who was born in the city of Philadelphia, but principally raised in the State of Virginia. He sustained the character of a good, moral, industrious man. He has left a wife and infant daughter to mourn his loss. MR. S. was at the time of his death in the employ of the Central Railroad, in the capacity of Engineer.

At Americus, on Saturday, 4th inst., Rev. JOHN W. TWITTY, of the Methodist Episcopal church, and Minister in Charge of the Americus Circuit. Brother Twitty had just attained his 34th year, and had been engaged in the active duties of the Ministry a little more than five years.

Issue of September 28, 1852

Funeral Notice – The friends and acquaintances of MR. J. C. EDWARDS and family, MRS. MARGARET WARNER, MR. GEORGE WARNER, and DR. CS. PUTNAM and family, are respectfully invited to attend the funeral of MR. BENJAMIN B. HOPKINS, from the dwelling of MR. J. C. EDWARDS, this morning at 10 o'clock.

Married – On the 2d ult., by DANIEL MCCOOK, Esq., at his residence, MR. JAMES G. RADFORD to MISS EMELINE PITTS – all of Wilkinson county.

On the same evening, by DANIEL MCCOOK, Esq., MR. WM. ETHEREDGE to MISS AMANDA SPENCE – all of Wilkinson county.

On the 2d inst., by W. B. SHEPHERD, Esq., MR. JAMES W. SCOTT to MISS MARTHA J. S. SHINHOLSER.

On the 8th ult., by JAMES BRANNON, Esq., MR. HUGH DICKS, to MISS MARY DAVIS – all of Wilkinson county.

Died – In Brooklyn, New York, on the 2d inst., at the residence of MR. WILLIAM PRENTISS, her son-in-law, MRS VIRGINIA HUNT, aged 60 years. For the last two years a resident of Macon.

At the residence of MR. ROBERT A. ALLEN, near Augusta, on Sunday 26th ult., MR. BENJAMIN B. HOPKINS, aged 76 years, formerly a citizen of Macon.

At Marietta on Friday the 24th inst., FREDERICK R. TARVER, Esq., of Twiggs county, in the 24th year of his age. Obituary hereafter.

Issue of October 5, 1852

Death of the DUKE OF WELLINGTON – The Canada brought advices of the death of the DUKE OF WELLINGTON. He died on the 16th ult., of Apoplexy. The DUKE was the fourth son of the Earl of Monington and was born at Dungan Castle, in the county of Meath, Ireland, on the 1st of May, 1769, consequently at the time of his death he was in his 84th year. He is succeeded in his vast estates and title by his eldest son, the MARQUIS OF DOURD.

Death of Gen. S. ARMSTRONG BAILEY – It is our painful duty to announce the decease of Gen. S. A. BAILEY. He died suddenly at his residence, in the vicinity of this city, on Sunday, the 26th inst., at half past eleven o'clock, A. M. The deceased was born, we believe, at Mount Zion, in the county of Hancock, in this State. He has for many years been a resident of this city, where in all his relations to society, he has maintained the highest reputation for integrity and honor.

Died – In this city, on the 16th ult., MISS MARTHA T. WILLIAMS, eldest daughter of REUBEN WILLIAMS, Esq. of Lee county, Georgia, in the 19th year of her age. Just two months previously, MISS W. had graduated at the Wesleyan Female College...

Issue of October 12, 1852

Married – at Pleasant Hill, on the 30th ult., by Rev. A. B. SMITH, MR. F. GIPSEY GODBEE, to MISS ROSALIE D., daughter of THOMAS J. DIXON, all of Burke county.

In Cobb county, on the 29th ult. by the Rev. B TOLLESON, MR. JNO. E. RAY, to MISS JANE WILMOUTH, all of Cobb county.

Near Columbus, on the 28th ult., by Rev. JAMES F. EVANS, MR. SAMUEL E. WHITAKER, of Baldwin county to MISS HENRIETTA, daughter of VAN LEONARD, Esq. of Muscogee county.

At Troy, on the 30th ult., MR. B. YOUNG to MISS AMANDA ALFORD, all of Harris county.

In Houston county, on the 25th ult.,, by Rev. L. J. ROBERT, MR. F. W. ROBERT, to MISS SARAH FRANCES PIERCE, all of Marietta, Ga.

Died – In Cobb county, on the 29th LEONARD WILLIS, a Revolutionary Soldier, aged 103 years and five months.

Died – In the city of Marietta, on the morning of the 24th ult., after an illness of twenty-five days, MR. FREDERICK R. TARVER, of Twiggs county, Ga., in the 25th year of his age.

Hon. E. A. HANNEGAN, of Indiana, who killed his brother-in-law, the gallant Capt. DUNCAN, in a drunken brawl some time since, is now clear from all legal proceedings. His case was brought before the Fountain (Ind.) Circuit Court, but the Grand Jury failed to find an indictment.

Death of Hon. W. H. HAYWOOD, formerly U. S. Senator from N. C. – We are deeply pained that this distinguished gentleman died at his residence in this city, on the7th inst. His disease was Cancer of the Tongue, with which he had been come time lingering.

Raleigh Register

Married – In Twiggs county, on the evening of the 30th ult. by Rev. HENRY BUNN, MR. JAMES T. GLOVER, to MISS GEORGIA ANN, daughter of JAMES BUNN, Esq.

In Pulaski county, on the 5th inst. by the Rev. H. BUNN, DR. VIRGIL H. WALKER, of Harris county, to MISS ANTOINETTE, daughter of DAVID WALKER.

In Lumpkin, Stewart county, on the 30th ult. by the Rev. C. A. FULLWOOD, MR. WM. M. BARNES to MISS SARAH E., daughter of STODDARD ROCKWELL, all of the above place.

In Washington, Wilkes county, 12th inst., by the Rev. MR. HABERSHAM, MR. TROUPE BUTLER, of Lee county to MISS A. C. ANDREWS, daughter of the Hon. GARNETT ANDREWS of the former place.

Died, in Talbotton, Ga. on the 8th inst. SARAH MARGARET, daughter of JOHN J. and MARY L. GROVES, in the 21st year of her age.

Twenty Dollars Reward – Stop the Runaways – Left my plantation on the night of the 21st September last, four miles east of Greenville, Meriwether county, Georgia, my two negro men, BEN and BROOKS. BEN is 30 years old, weighs 170 lbs., black, has a thick beard, slow of speech, a down look and shows the whites of his eyes a good deal when he looks at you; whites tinged yellow, and has an humble cast. BROOKS is 25 years old, copper colored, very intelligent, quick spoken, has a soft pleasant voice, of middle stature, weighs 160 lbs., has several scars on him, one on the left side of his throat, one on the back of his right hand and arm 8 inches long, extending down between the middle and ring fingers, others on his body and head done with a knife and stick. Said negroes if not decoyed off by a white man, will likely make for the gold mines in North Carolina. They may have free passes.

WM. D. TINSLEY

Issue of October 26, 1852

Death of DANIEL WEBSTER

Death of Col. JOHN G. GAMBLE – We are deeply pained to announce, says the Tallahassee Sentinel of the 19th inst., the sudden death of Col. JOHN G. GAMBLE, which took place at Neomathla, his residence in this county, early this morning. We learn from a servant that Col. G. had risen, apparently in his usual health, and walked to the door of his house, when he suddenly fell down and expired. This melancholy news in town awakens universal surprise and concern.

Issue of November 2, 1852

Died, on the 14th ult., in Twiggs county, at the residence of his mother, JOSHUA S. JOHNSON, in the 17th year of his age.

On the 24th ult. JOSEPH DUNCAN, son of GEORGE F. and LEONORA E. COOPER, aged seven months and one day.

Issue of November 9, 1852

A Boy Shot By His Father – We do not remember when our feelings were more touched with an account of a catastrophe, than on listening a few days since, to the relation of the circumstances of MR. JOHN WILLIAMS of Covington township, in this county, mistaking his son for a deer, and shooting him, on the 11th inst. MR. WILLIAMS left his house in company with MR. JAS. PARRY, for the purpose of showing him the way through the woods to a point for which MR. PARRY had started, and took with him a loaded gun. After going about 400 yards from his house, he thought he saw a deer, and taking close aim, fired. His horror can better be imagined than described, on instantly hearing his little son, ISAAC, a fine boy of about 12 years of age, cry out, "Father, why did you shoot me?" The father exclaimed to his companion, "Oh! Did ever man shoot his boy before?"

Both men ran and met the boy approaching them, about twenty yards from the place where he was shot. It was observed that the ball had entered the back, near the shoulder blade, and passing through the body, passed out a little on one side of the center of the breast. No hope was entertained that the boy would live half an hour. MR. PARRY was so confused and confounded, that he knew little of what had passed, and only recollects that it was proposed to carry the boy into the house, about 400 years distant, to which the little fellow objected, and asked that he might lie down. With his father's coat for a bed, his request was granted, when he cast an anxious look at his frantic parent, and said, "Father, you will bury me on the farm, won't you?" Immediately, MR. PARRY hastened for a physician, and on his way gave notice to a neighbor, who hurried to the spot and carried the boy into the house against his will.

The physician arrived, and believed the boy would not survive through the night. He did, however, and as late as one week after, when we last heard from him, was doing well, the physician and friends strong in the hope that he would recover, having come to the conclusion that the ball did not touch a vital part. The little fellow is cheerful and patient, breaths well, has good appetite, and talks freely. No doubt many a hearty prayer has been offered up to Heaven for his recovery. Poor little fellow, may he be restored, and yet be a blessing to his deeply sorrowing parent. The lad was gathering chesnuts in the woods. The color of his clothes resembled that of a deer, and the wristband of one shirt sleeve projecting a little below the coat sleeve, the father mistook it for the end of a deer's tail, which is frequently white, and fired.

Wilks. Adv.

Married – On Wednesday morning, the 3d inst. at Fenins Bridge, Jefferson county, by the Rev. MR. VERDAREE, AUGUSTUS A. QUARTERMAN, Esq. of Liberty county, to MISS ANNIE M. daughter of B. H. MOULTRIE, of the former place.

In Augusta on the 28th ult., by the Rev. MR. HUGHES, MR. HENRY DAMM and MISS LOUISA WELLAUER, only daughter of GEORGE WELLAUER all of said city.

In Columbus county, on the 28th ult., by the Rev. MR. COLLINS, MR. R. R. LEWIS and MISS M. CHAPPE LEAR, all of said county.

Near Cassville, on the 5th ult., FRANCES C. SHROPSHIRE, Esq. and MISS MARY A. eldest daughter of Hon. AUGUSTUS A. WRIGHT.

In Griffin, on the 24th ult., by the Rev. BUCKNER, Maj. P. A. LAWSON, to MISS JULIA A. PARKS.

Died – In Athens, on the 12th ult., LAURA ROOTES, youngest child of Governor and Mrs. HOWELL COBB, aged 10 months and 11 days.

At Gordon, on Saturday last, JAMES M. FOLSOM, Esq., a native of New Hampshire, aged about 45 years, but for a number of years a citizen of Georgia.

Twenty Dollars Reward – Will be paid for the apprehension and delivery to me of my negro girl CAROLINE, who has been a runaway for several months. She is quite a good looking girl, with a full face and full head of hair, generally well combed, and she usually dresses well, is five feet five and a half inches high, of a ginger-cake color and well proportioned. When sewing she does not generally use her forefinger on her left hand. She may probably change her name and say that she is hired out. I have good reasons to believe she is either in Macon or its vicinity.

B. TAYLOR

Issue of November 16, 1852

Tribute of Respect to the Memory of DANIEL WEBSTER.

Married – On the 28th ult. by Rev. J. C. SHARPE, MR. JOHN BURK, to MISS SARAH J. CARSWELL, both of Wilkinson co., Ga.

In Haynesville, Houston county, on the 10th inst. by the Rev. E. P. BURCH, MR. OLIVER R. PHELPS, of Forsyth, and MISS EUGENIA C. LANIER of Haynesville.

On Tuesday, 9th inst. by Rev. A. BUCKNER, at the residence of GEORGE PROTHRO, Pike county, MR. FIELDING FLEMISTER of Griffin, to MISS MARTHA PROTHRO of the former place.

Obituary – Died, at his residence in Houston county, Ga., on the 6th inst., WILLIAM AVERA, Esq. in the 49th year of his age. MR. AVERA was born in Washington county, in this State, but has been for the last twenty years a citizen of Houston county. The deceased was a victim of Typhoid Fever, he was sick but a few days, and bore his severe affliction with great patience. He died calmly without a struggle...He has left a wife and a large family of children...

Died in this city, on the 9th inst., MR. ALFRED C. MOREHOUSE, aged 35 years, a native of Syracuse, New York, but for the last twelve years a resident of this city, and at the time of his death a Representative from the county of Bibb in the Georgia legislature.

Died, on the 30th ult. in the city of Savannah, MR. EDMUND W. BAILEY, son of JOHN BAILEY, Esq. of this county, in the 26th year of his age...The disease which terminated the life of MR. BAILEY, thus early in the morning of life, was generated by exposure, while conducting as superintendent, the works of his uncle DR. ROBERT COLLINS, contractor of the Brunswick Canal.

Issue of November 23, 1852

Obituary – Died – at his own residence in Twiggs county, on Saturday morning, November 7th, HENRY FAULK, JR., son of MARK FAULK, deceased, in the 26th year of his age.

Died, at Leicester, Mass., November 11th, the Hon. DAVID HENSHAW, formerly Secretary of the Navy.

Died – In Thomaston, Upson county, on Thursday 28th October, MRS. EPHATHA C. wife of WILLIAM D. WOODSON, and daughter of the late SAMUEL BOWDRE, of Columbia county, Ga. Several years ago the deceased united herself to the Methodist Episcopal church...

Died – On Sunday, 7th inst., at Springfield, Mass MR. LEWIS W. BABCOCK, aged 28 years, for several years a resident of this city.

Died – In Knoxville, Crawford county, on Monday, the 15th inst., Major RICHARD W. ELLIS, an old and much esteemed citizen of Crawford county, in the 70th year of his age. Major ELLIS resided for many years in this city. In his death the Baptist church, of which he was a member for the last thirty years, has lost one of its brightest and most useful members and the community in which he lived one if its most worthy citizens.

Stop the Runaway – On Friday or Saturday of the late Fair at Macon, a man named BENJAMIN REED, left the Fair Ground in charge of my mules and wagon. REED claims to be a Spaniard, is about 55 or 60 years old, about 5 feet 6 inches high, copper colored, straight hair and grey eyes, speaks the Spanish, English and Italian languages. On his left arm is printed with India ink, the Flag of the United States, an Anchor and the figure of a Female. The wagon is a two horse with iron axles, box body and deep red standards; the cover somewhat old, and the whip what is termed a Kentucky horse whip. In the wagon was a considerable quantity of bed clothing and other articles____ ____ _____out at the Fair. One of the mules is a light bay mare, well made, with a scar on her left hip, between 4 and 6 inches long, made by a knife; on the opposite hip is a small grey spot; her age is a little over three years. The other is a dark horse mule, a little larger than the mare, and appears to limp when walking, supposed to be tolerable old. A liberal reward will be paid for the apprehension of REED, or for the recovery of the mules and wagon, and any information thankfully received. My address is Delrey, Upson county, Georgia.

HARVEY TICE

Runaway or Stolen – About the last day of the Fair, my negro girl FRANCES or FANNY about 20 years old, a copper colored, mulatto woman, very likely. She has probably been decoyed off, or harbored by some white person about the city. A reasonable reward will be paid for her apprehension and delivery to myself, or the Jailor of Bibb county. If harbored I will pay a liberal reward for proof to convict the person harboring her.

DAVID JAMESON

Issue of November 30, 1852

The Hon. JOHN SERGEANT died at Philadelphia, on Tuesday night, the 23d inst., in his 73d year, and the Hon. WALTER FORWARD, at Pittsburg, on Wednesday, the 24th inst., in his 65th year.

Ex-Governor SHULTZ of Pennsylvania, died at his residence on the 19th inst. He had lived to a good old age.

Married – On the 25th November by the Rev. T. F. MONTGOMERY, of LaGrange, Ga. JAMES D. FREDERICK of Marshallville, Ga. to MISS ELIZA A. FELDER, of Orangeburgh, S. C.

Died – In Houston county, on the 21st November at a quarter past 1 o'clock, MR. JAS. GATES. MR. G. was born in Edgefield District, S. C. on the 15th December 1804. He moved to this State and was a resident of Jones county for a number of years, when he removed to Bibb county, where, after a few years residence, he was elected Tax Collector, and subsequently Sheriff of the county, which office he filled to the satisfaction of the community, and finally removed to Houston county, at all of which places he enjoyed the confidence of his fellow citizens and the warm attachment of a large circle of friends. He was a member of the Anti-Missionary Baptist church for eighteen years, and had filled the office of Deacon for several years. He was ever regarded as a worthy man and a Christian... He confidently expected death several days before it came. He gathered his family about him, and in the most touching manner affirmed his love for them and gave them parting advice...

Issue of December 7, 1852

MR. SAMUEL PARKER, seventy years of age, has just married his sixth wife at Cincinnati. Since his first he has always married a widow, and never remained a widower longer than six months at one time.

Casualty – The Alabama Journal of
the 30th ult. says: "The recent rain has been productive of many accidents, besides the loss of mails, bridges and stock, have been lost on the various routes, and we have the melancholy duty to perform of recording the loss of human life. On Saturday night an attempt was made to cross the Tallapoosa at Judkins' Ferry, by MR. THOMAS MOULTON, of this place, and a MR. ROUSE OF Westumpka, in a batteau, managed by a negro belonging to MR. WINTER of this place. In the passage the boat was upset, and MR. ROUSE and the boy were drowned. MR. MOULTON having been for several hours on a snag, succeeded in reaching the shore."

Death from a Rifle Shot – The Chronicle & Sentinel of Sunday morning says, we were yesterday shown a private letter from a gentleman in Lawrenceville, Ga., to his friend in this city, detailing the particulars of the shooting of

WILLIAM S. WINN by ARCHIBALD A. DUNLAP, both of Gwinnett county.

It appears that WINN had, for some time, carried on an improper intercourse with the wife of DUNLAP, of which he was cognizant. On the 23d inst., he saw W. pass his place, soon after which he repaired to his house and found that his wife was missing. He picked up his rifle and went in pursuit; and overtook them in the woods, not far distant, and fired upon WINN, the ball entered the abdomen and passing out at the right hip, of which he died in about 30 hours.

Married – In Crawford county, on the 9th ult. by Rev. GEORGE F. PIERLE, J. C. LONGSTREET, Esq. to MISS M. A. LAMAR, daughter of the late Hon. L. Q. C. LAMAR.

In Crawford county, on the 28th ult., by JOHN F. TAYLOR, Esq. MR. WILLIS W. TAYLOR, to MISS FRANCIS M. FOWLER, all of Crawford county, Ga.

In this city, on Sunday morning last, by the Rev. MR. BROCK, MR. JOHN L. COPE of Savannah to MISS VIRGINIA SULLIVAN, of this city.

Obituary – In Houston county, on the 29th ult. MRS. MARY JOINER, consort of Capt. MEREDITH JOINER, in the 69(?) th year of her age. The deceased was a native of North Carolina and her aged husband were among the pioneer settlers of this county, having moved to the place where she died. MRS. J. had been a consistent member of the Church of the Living God for about 54(?) years.

On Saturday afternoon, Nov. 20th at the residence of his uncle, BENJ. BRYAN, in Houston county, JOSEPH M. BRYAN, son of BLACKSHEAR and TEMPERANCE BRYAN deceased, in the 25th year of his age...

Died – In St. Mary's, Camden county, on the 28th ult., MRS. TERESA DE WITT, aged 88 years.

Issue of December 14, 1852

Death of JOHN O'KEEFE -We are called upon to record another sudden death by violence in our midst. Last Saturday night, about 12 o'clock, MR. O'KEEFE, while walking up the side walk, near the Washington Hall, was assaulted by an individual of the name of _____ BOYD, and almost instantly killed after the infliction of five or six wounds from a dirk knife. The offender having been promptly arrested and turned over to the judicial tribunals, we forbear to make further remarks upon the character of the transaction. MR. O'KEEFE has been a citizen of Macon for twenty years pursuing creditably for most of that time, the occupation of a schoolmaster, and was noted for his quiet, retiring and inoffensive character. Boyd, we believe, is a journeyman saddler, in the employment of W. T. Mix & Co. of this place.

Burglaries – During the past week the store of MR. G. EHRLERB was broken into, and robbed of a considerable amount of clothing and other articles, and on the same night the cellar of MR. JAMES S. GRAYBILL'S Family Grocery was robbed of considerable amount of provisions. We understand that on Saturday night a portion of the articles were found in a shop on Cotton Avenue.

Married – on the 7th inst., by Judge STURDEVANT, JOHN A. W. M'CANTS, Esq. of Butler, Taylor county, Ga., Clerk of the Superior Court of Taylor county, to MISS MARTHA A. BATEMAN, of Marion county.

On the 18th ult., at the house of NATHAN CHILDERS, in Crawford county, Ga. by CHARLES H. WALKER, Esq., JOEL T. HANCOCK to ELIZABETH P. CHILDERS.

In Vineville, on the 9th inst., by Rev. WM. RICHARDS, of S. C., MR. S. P. RICHARDS to MISS SARAH F. VAN VALKENBURG.

In Monroe county on the 1st ult., by Rev. SENECA G. BRAGG, L. M. DEMICK to MISS ELIZABETH ULTON, all of this city.

In Vineville, on the 6th inst., by Rev. MR. MYERS, MR. WM. M. WALKER of Burke county, to MISS CAROLINE M. RAWLS.

Died – In Jones county, Ga. on the 9th of December, 1852, MRS. MARY CARD, in the 71st year of her age, of protracted illness, which she bore with Christian fortitude. The deceased was an exemplary member of the Baptist church for nearly forty years. She leaves an aged husband, four children and quite a number of grandchildren...

Issue of December 21, 1852

Fire – On Sunday evening about 6 o'clock, we were startled by the cry of fire and found it proceeded from the dwelling of MRS. JOHN T. LAMAR, on Pine Street, which was entirely consumed. The spread of the fire was prevented by cutting down and removing a small kitchen, and by the active exertions of our citizens. MRS. LAMAR'S furniture was all saved, though somewhat damaged in the hurry of removal. We learn that MRS. LAMAR'S dwelling was insured in the Southern Mutual Insurance Company at one thousand dollars. The fire is supposed to be the work of an incendiary.

Negro Stealing – The Athens Banner of Thursday last says, MR. EDWARD LAMPKIN, of Union Point, brought to this place on Saturday last, a man by the name of AVERY PERKINS, and three negro fellows, supposed to be from 25 to 30 years of age, under a strong ground of suspicion that the negroes had been stolen by PERKINS, in whose possession they were.

Perkins sold two of them to LAMKIN and WM. A. CARR, at rates so low fortified by an examination of the negroes. One of the negroes by the name of SAM, says he belongs to a MR. AUSTIN, at Atlanta. JEF says he belongs to ISHMY BLACK of Putnam, about 13 miles from Madison, Morgan county. JIM says he belongs to MRS. SARAH AKRY, near Stone Mountain in DeKalb.

PERKINS and the negroes have all been sent to the county jail at Watkinsville.

Smallpox in Talbot – We regret to hear, says the Literary Vademeeum, of the 16th inst., that Maj. JOHN W. G. SMITH died at his residence in Talbot county, a few days since, from Small Pox. He encountered the disease while on a recent visit to Montgomery, Ala., from a child who was in the cars with him, and who unknown to Maj. SMITH, had the disease. Maj. SMITH was a gentleman of high standing in society, and universally respected and esteemed by all who knew him. Of refined and sympathetic feelings he fell a victim to the innate goodness of his heart, for in attempting to relieve the sufferings of a helpless child he contracted the disease which terminated his existence. He represented, a few years since, the counties of Marion and Talbot in the senatorial branch of our State Legislature, and at the time of his death was Inspector of the 2d Brigade, 10th Division, G. M. He has left four orphan children, together with numerous friends, to mourn his loss.

We understand that great precaution has been taken to prevent the spread of the disease, and as yet no new cases have occurred. All communication between persons at the house where the patient died and the citizens, has been interdicted, and one of the physicians who attended him, and the family of Maj. SMITH, are not allowed to leave the house. We hope the disease has been arrested.

Hon. EDWARD C. MARSHALL, member of Congress from California, was married in Cincinnati, on the 29th ult. to MISS JOSEPHINE, daughter of ROBERT CHALFRANT, Esq.

JOHN ANDERSON, one of the oldest citizens of Cincinnati, died on the 4th inst. He was born in Ireland in January, 1751, fought in the Irish rebellion, landed in Cincinnati in 1800, and at the time of his death was nearly 101 years of age.

MRS. JAMISON, a niece of General FRANKLIN PIERCE, was married in Boston on Thursday to MR. HENSHAW. The President-elect and his lady were present at the wedding.

Married – In Twiggs county, on the 5th inst. by Rev. H. H. BUNN, MR. JOHN FAULK to MISS VICTORIA A. daughter of the late Col. HENRY SOLOMON of Twiggs county.

At the M. S. church, on the 19th inst., by the Rev. G. __. HANCOCK, MR. OSCAR P. FITZGERALD, to MISS SARAH ___., daughter of B. F. GRIFFIN, Esq. all of Macon.

In Montgomery, Ala., on Sunday evening, 12th inst. by the Rev. I. T. TICHENOR, MR. P. A. KNIGHT, to MISS ___. A. FLOYD.

Died – In Leon county, Florida, on the 27th November, after a short illness, NICHOLAS LLOYD, Esq. in the 65th year of his age. He was a native of North Carolina and resided for many years in Twiggs county, in this State, from whence he removed to Florida about fifteen years since. He has left a wife and a large circle of friends to mourn his death.

On the 9ᵗʰ inst., of Small Pox at his residence in Talbot county, Maj. JOHN W. G. SMITH, in his 43d year. The deceased was born in Jones county and moved to Talbot county about fifteen years since, there lived honored and respected. He leaves four children, many relatives and friends to mourn his premature death. He contracted the disease on a late trip to Montgomery, Ala.

In Hamilton, Canada, a week or two since, MR. ROBERT BOLES died very suddenly from the shock _____ by being informed that some mischievous person had caused his funeral notice to be printed.

Issue of December 28, 1852

The Oldest Printer – The oldest living printer in the United States is a man named DERLYOR DORLY, in Yorkville, S. C. He worked with JOHN RUSSELL on the Boston Sentinel, over half a century ago, and he yet sets type by candle light and is 94 years of age.

Senator PEARCE Struck by a Lady – During a debate in the U. S. Senate on Monday last, a parasol dropped from the hand of a lady in the gallery, which fell, point downward, on the head of the Hon. MR. PEARCE, of Maryland, cutting him severely but not seriously. MR. P., after some time, resumed his seat in the Senate.

Issue of January 4, 1853

Death of Gen. JOSEPH BENNETT. We regret to learn the death of General JOSEPH BENNETT, by a fall from the second story of a building on Third street, about 10o'clock on Sunday night, from the effects of which he died between 3 and 4 o'clock on Monday morning. Gen BENNETT was a native of New York and came to this city in the year 1823 with one of the first stocks of Goods ever opened in the city. He was afterwards elected Brigadier General of this

Brigade, and subsequently a member of the Legislature from this county.

AMOS LAWRENCE died at Boston on Friday.

Death of Judge TAYLOR – We regret to learn says the Columbus Times of the 29th December, that a private letter was received in the city yesterday announcing the decease of the Hon. WM. TAYLOR, of Randolph county, Judge of the South Western Circuit of this State.

Died – At his residence, in Baker county, on the 25th ult., Major L. S. BROOKIN, aged about 38 years, formerly of Hancock county. Major BROOKIN was a planter; a good citizen, a kind neighbor and friend and was much respected by all who knew him. He was for several years Sheriff of Hancock county.

Death of Commander DALE – JOHN M. DALE, a commander in the United States Navy, died in Philadelphia last week. He had been in the service for more than forty years, having entered the Navy on the 18th of June, 1812.

A Proclamation by HOWELL COBB, Governor of Said State. Whereas, I have received official information that a murder was committed on the 26th inst., in the county of Bibb, upon the body of AARON BLALOCK, by GEORGE MINCHEW, and that the said MINCHEW has fled from justice.
I have thought proper therefore, to issue this, my Proclamation, hereby offering a reward of One Hundred and Fifty Dollars, to any person or persons, who may apprehend and deliver the said GEORGE MINCHEW to the Sheriff of said county of Bibb. And I do moreover charge and require, all officers of this State, both Civil and Military, to be vigilant in endeavoring to apprehend and

deliver, the said GEORGE MINCHEW, in order that he may be tried for the offence with which he stands charged.

HOWELL COBB

Issue of January 11, 1853

Death of SAMUELJ. RAY – On the 5th instant, at the residence of DR. H. K. GREEN in this city, SAMUELJ. RAY, Esq., the Senior Editor of the Georgia Telegraph, breathed his last. MR. RAY, was born August 15, 1814 in Moore county, North Carolina, but removed in early manhood to the State of Georgia, where he constantly resided to the period of his decease. (long article).

Frightful Railroad Accident – Boston Jan. 6 – A frightful railroad accident occurred today on the Boston and Maine Railroad. President PIERCE and lady were among the passengers and are reported to be much injured. Their only son, a lad ten years old, was instantly killed.

Affray – On the night of Wednesday last, says the Columbus Times of the 7th inst., two men named JOHN CALVIN and WM. STAINS, of Girard, Ala., we are informed, made a murderous assault upon E. B. W. SPIVEY, of this city, with pistols. In the mele, MR. SPIVEY'S son brought him a double barrelled gun, with which he shot both the assailants. We are told that they are both in a dying condition. MR. SPIVEY received a ball in the hand, another on the head. He is not seriously injured.

Negro Stealing – The Federal Union of the 4th inst. says, MESSRS. SEARLY and JENKINS of this city, arrested one GEO. M. JONES on Thursday last, near Monticello, who had some twelve negroes in his possession, one of which escaped after he was apprehended. Said negroes belong to MR. P. BAILEY, of Double Wells, Warren county, Ga.,

THOS. MORMON, of Harris county and DR. W. A. JARRATT, of Baldwin county, excepting four owned by the said JONES.

JONES had encamped near this city for several days prior to the absence of DR. JARRATT'S boy, and it was suspected at once that he had stolen him, having had the boy in his tent several times, and having been known to have had a consultation with said boy. MESSRS. SEARCY and JENKINS were at once put on track of JONES, and arrested him without much trouble. JONES was fired at, the ball grazing his scalp. The white man and negroes are all confined in Jail at this place. MESSRS. SEARCY and JENKINS deserve much praise for their vigilance in arresting the said JONES.

Married, on the 4th inst. by Judge KEELIN COOK, SAMUEL T. CHAMBLISS, to MISS AMANDA GILBERT, all of this county.

On the 26th ult. by Rev. MR. E. QUIGLEY, MR. MILTON WRIGHT, of Oglethorpe, to MISS CATHARINE ANN DOYLE, of this city.

On Thursday evening, 30th inst., in Forsyth, by Rev. SAMUEL ANTHONY, JOSEPH R. BANKS, Esq. to MISS CARRIE S. SHEPHENS.

In this city on Sunday morning last, by SOLOMON R. JOHNSON, Esq. MR WIAT W. JOHNSON, to MRS. SARAH F. CARSONS.

On the 5th of January in Pulaski county, by Hon. S. M. MANNING, MR. JNO. H. BRANTLY, JR. of Houston county, to MISS EUOFAIR J. MCGRIFF, of the former county.

At the residence of JOHN MCKAY, on Saturday 25th Dec. by MR. H. M. NIXON, Esq., MR. FRANCIS HILL, Esq. to MISS M. E. POSTELL, all of Houston county.

Also, at the same time and place, as above, by MR. H. M. NIXON, Esq. DR. JOHN MCMILLAN to MISS ELLEN LAMAR, daughter of MRS. SARAH LAMAR, of Houston county.

Issue of January 18, 1853

A Hoax – We last week published the marriage of FRANCIS HILL, Esq., to MISS M. E. POSTELL, also the marriage of DR. JOHN MCMILLON to MISS ELLEN LAMAR. We have since learned that no such marriages took place. In justice to the parties and ourselves, we will state that we received a letter requesting us to publish the above marriages, and thinking the letter to be genuine, we complied with the request of the writer. We now have the letter in our possession, which any of the parties can see by calling on us.

Further Particulars of the Accident to Gen. PIERCE and Family.
We gather from the New York papers some additional particulars of the railroad accident by which Gen. PIERCE and wife were injured and their son killed:
The train was composed of a baggage and passenger car. The exact cause of the accident is not definitely ascertained' one of the axletrees is supposed to have broken; some say it was the journal on which the wheel plays. The day was very cold – the thermometer pointed at zero – and the accident was doubtless owing to the frost in the iron works of the ill- fated car.
MRS. PIERCE and the deceased son had been absent four weeks on a visit to relatives in Boston and Andover. The accident happened near the latter place. Gen. PIERCE went to Boston Tuesday morning, and with them attended

the funeral of MRS. PIERCE'S uncle, Hon. AMOS LAWRENCE on the same afternoon. They remained at MR. AIKEN'S in Andover, whose lady is a sister of MRS. PIERCE, and were expected to return in the evening.

The train in which they went, left Boston at noon Thursday, and the accident happened just after it left the Andover depot, twenty miles from Boston, at about one. They had not been in the cars five minutes.

Gen. PIERCE after the accident appeared composed but MRS. PIERCE was taken away in a very high state of mental anguish. Her screams were agonizing. The little boy was their only child, an elder brother having died some ten years ago.

At the time of the accident Gen. PIERCE was conversing with MR. YOUNG, the superintendent of the new mills at Lawrence. Professor PACKARD, a relative of General PIERCE, was in company with MRS. PIERCE and her son, and the party occupied the forward part of the car, which was divided in the middle. They were all thrown in a heap, on over another. Master Pierce lay upon the floor of the car, with his skull frightfully fractured. The cap which he had worn had fallen off, and was filled with blood and brains.

A little girl of MR. NEWALL, of Hillsborough, had her foot crushed, and it must be amputated. MRS. NEWALL was badly injured, and MR. NEWALL had a leg broken. MR. HORACE CHILDS, bridge builder, of Henniker, was badly but not seriously bruised. Several women were severely bruised.

The car is said to have broken near the middle. The baggage car in front was not thrown off. A Brakeman stood on the end of it and witnessed the accident unharmed.

A dispatch, dated Concord, Thursday evening, says: Considerable apprehensions felt here lest this melancholy fatality may prove serious in its consequences to MRS. PIERCE. She has been for several years in delicate health, caused partly by the loss of her first child. The boy killed by this accident was almost idolized by his mother and father.

The announcement of the accident in the New Hampshire Legislature created intense excitement. Neither General PIERCE nor his lady received much physical injury, though both of them are overwhelmed with grief.

The Tennessee papers announce the death of Hon. DANIEL L. BARRENGER, a distinguished citizen of that State, and formerly a member of Congress from North Carolina.

The Illness of Vice-President King. A letter from Washington, dated the 6th inst., says: Hon. W. R. KING has made his will. He was born in 1786; owns 5,000 acres of land in one body in Dallas county, Alabama, and upward of one hundred slaves. His entire estate is worth about $150,000. He is a humane master. He told me some years since that he never sold but one slave in his life, and he was compelled to sell him because he was a terror to the neighborhood. Col. KING cannot possibly recover. His physician has sounded his lungs with the stethoscope, and declared that one of his lungs is entirely gone, and the other partly so. Col. K's niece, MRS. ELLIS, is with him.

Death of HAMBLIN, the Actor. The New York papers announce the death of THOMAS HAMBLIN, Esq., in that city, which event took place on the night of the 8th inst., about twenty minutes before eleven o'clock, at his home, 416 Broom street. The cause was brain fever, with which he was attacked on the previous Monday evening, up to which time he was in perfect health.

MR. HAMBLIN first appeared in this country on the 18th of April, 1826, in Philadelphia, in the character of MacBeth...

A Centenarian in Jail. "A man named JOSEPH HIDE is in Prison in Cincinnati, who was born at sea, between England and the United States, on the 10th of June, 1753, and was consequently ninety-nine last June. He has resided at Cincinnati, excepting some trifling absences, for more than fifty-six years. On the 17th of August, 1851, his sight was affected by a stroke of lightning, since which time he has been able to distinguish objects only sufficiently well to find his way through the streets without a guide. During the last fourteen years he has spent some portion of every year in the poor house, maintaining himself, when not there, by sawing wood, selling herbs, and other similar occupations. As we have said, he is now confined to the county jail on the charge of vagrancy, his only crime being old age, blindness and inability to labor." Athens Banner

$10 Reward – Runaway from the subscriber in the city of Macon, on the 13th December last, a negro man named FRANK. He is about 45 years old, bright black, had on a new linsy sack coat, white pants, and an old white hat; he has a scar on the back of his right hand, also a scar on the left ear, a part of the scar may be seen immediately back of the left ear on the head. He was seen 8 or 10 days past in the neighborhood of THOMAS B. GREEN, in Upson county. I will give the above reward for his apprehension and confinement.

Issue of Jan 25, 1853

Ex-Alderman CLAYTON died in New York on Sunday, from injuries received by the explosion of gas.

Married, on the 20th inst., by Judge DAVIS, MR. JAMES B. WALL, of Twiggs county, Ga. to MISS REBECCA A. daughter of JOHN H. LOWE, Esq. of Bibb county.

On the 11th inst., in Dooly county, Ga., by the Rev. H. C. HORNADY, MR. J. T. JACKSON, of Lee county, to MISS LOUISA ANTOINETT, eldest daughter of M. J. WEST, of the former county.

On the 13th inst., by E. H. HICKS, Esq. MR. G. A. CULVERHOUSE, OF Crawford, to MISS SARAH A. M. MCMANUS, of Bibb county.

On Sunday, the 23d inst., by STERLING TUCKER, Esq. MR. RANSOM DOWNS, to MISS EVELINE RILEY, all of Bibb county.

Issue of February 1, 1853

Died, on the 8th of January, 1853, at his late residence in Jones county, ALEXANDER J. HUNT, in the 46th year of his age. He fell as it were in the prime of his manhood, a prey to paralysis, with which he was struck on the Sunday previous.

Issue of February 8, 1853

Married, in this city, on the 31st Jan. by Rev. S.LANDRUM, MR. W. W. RICHARDS, to MISS SARAH F. WAGNON.

Tribute of Respect to THOMAS B. J. LAMAR

Obituary – Departed this life, in Lee county, Ga., on the 12th ult. in the 22nd year of her age, REBECCA E. MCCLENDON, consort of JONATHAN MCCLENDON, and daughter of JOHN G. and MARY S. RAINES.

Died, in Twiggs county, on the 1st inst., RICHARD DESHAZO, in the 52nd year of his age. The deceased had his faults as other men; but it can be truly said of him that he was an honest man.

F.

Issue of February 15, 1853

Married – In Jones county on 3rd inst., by the Hon. JOSEPH DAY, MR. FRANKLIN J. WALKER, to MISS HENRIETTA M. ASKEW, daughter of BENJAMIN A. ASKEW., Esq. all of Jones county.

Issue of February 22, 1853

A double murder was recently committed on board a flat boat in the Mississippi river, two men having charge of the boat being found with their skulls horribly crushed, and a large sum of money missing. A man named SIMMONS has been arrested at Louisville and confessed to the murder. Over $2500 of the money was found in his possession.

MR. FULLER, of Washington, who was recently shot by Capt. SCHAUMBURG, is in such improved condition that the chances now are in favor of his final recovery.

Two naval officers named NELSON and POLLOCK, have been arrested by order of Secretary of the Navy at Washington, on suspicion of being about to fight a duel.

Married, in Twiggs county, on the 13th instant, at the residence of MRS. F. SOLOMON, by the Rev. H. BUNN, Esq. MR. C. R. FAULK to MISS J. M. E. SOLOMON, daughter of MRS. F. SOLOMON, all of Twiggs county.

In Vineville on the 17th inst., by the Rev. E. H. MYERS, LUCIUS M. LAMAR, Esq., to MISS MARY F. daughter of MRS. CAROLINE RAWLS.

Died – In Savannah on the 10th inst., CATHERINE, only daughter of ISAAC G. and CAROLINE E. SEYMOUR, formerly of this city, now of New Orleans. Her remains lie in Rose Hill cemetery.

Atrocious Murder – A murder of the most atrocious kind, was committed in this county on last Saturday, by MR.. ARMSTEAD STOKES, on the body of JAMES HENLY. We give the particulars as correct as we have been able to ascertain them. MR. STOKES invited MR. HENLY to his house to assist him in the raising of a building; after the raising, he then invited him to dinner. Immediately after dinner he asked HENLY to take a short walk with him; they had not proceeded very far, when STOKES drew a knife, and without a moments warning plunged it to his heart, thereby causing instant death. MR. S. was under the influence of liquor. He was immediately arrested and brought before the Magistrate of the District, and after a careful examination was committed to jail to await his trial at our next Superior Court.

The deceased was a man of large family, and highly esteemed by all who knew him. In this sad event eight children, six girls and two small boys have been bereft of their only source of support. May He who feeds the young ravens, watch over and provide for the afflicted orphans. Washington (Ga.) Gazette

Issue of March 1, 1853

Buried Alive – Miraculous Rescue. On the 5th inst., at MR. MCC__ __VELSVILLE, Morgan county, Ohio, THOMAS CARTER, descended, by means of a ladder, into a well, thirty-five feet in depth, with the intention of securing some of the curbing that had been giving away. He had scarcely got down before he discovered that the whole above him was about caving in, and he began rapidly to ascend the ladder. He got up to within sixteen feet of the top, and there was caught by an immense body of sand, which filled all the space below and above him.

The citizens rallied to the spot and forthwith began digging him out, when it was discovered that there was a small aperture left, along the side of the ladder, through which they happily found that air could penetrate. They called and found the poor man able to talk, and he, in anticipation of their failure to get him out alive, instructed some of his friends how to arrange his business. Finally, they reached him, unharmed, from what all supposed a hopeless grave.

Married, on the 27th February, by S. LANDRUM, MR. F. L. HENRY, to MISS D. F. LEABETTER, all of this city.

Issue of March 8, 1853

The Hon. GEORGE BRIGGS was arrested at Washington on Saturday night for the late assault on Postmaster HUBBARD, on complaint of a private citizen and held to bail in the sum of $2000.

Married, in Houston county, on the 24th instant, by B. F. MOORE, Esq., MR. JOHN Q. GRIFFIN, of Minden, La. to MISS LOUISA A. daughter of WM. ALLEN, of Houston.

At Baltimore, on Feb. 15th, by the Rev. DR. ATKINSON, Lieut. D. R. JONES, U. S. Army, to MISS REBECCA, daughter of Col. J. P. TAYLOR, U. S. Army.

Obituary – Died at his residence near Marion in Twiggs county, on Friday morning, 11th February CHARLES C. WHITEHEAD, Esq. aged about 42 years.

Died in Harris county, February 13th, MRS. SUSAN H. CHOATE, wife of MR. JACOB T. CHOATE, formerly a resident of Vineville. MRS. CHOATE had been long a member of the Methodist church and her death was peaceful.

Departed this life, in Jones county, Ga., on the 5th ultimo, at the residence of her son, THOMAS S. HUMPHREY, MRS. MARY HUMPHREYS, in the 81st year of her age.

Died in Houston county, on the 26th inst., of inflammation of the tongue, MR. THOMAS HARDISON, aged about 22 years.

Issue of March 15, 1853

Married, on the 13th inst., by Rev. G. H. HANCOCK, MR. CHARLES H. ROGERS, to MISS LAURA A. RICHARDS, daughter of ALEX. RICHARDS, all of Macon.

Died, on the 3d February, at his residence near Montpelier Springs, in Monroe county, JOHN BROWN, Esq., in the 79th year of his age. MR. B. was one of the first settlers of Monroe county, and was much esteemed and respected by all who knew him.

On Wednesday morning, 9th inst., after a lingering illness, MR. JOHN P. EVANS, aged 53 years. MR. E. was a native of Rochester, New Hampshire, and for some time a resident in Charlestown, Massachussets. He has resided in Macon over 22 years, and at his demise was one of the oldest citizens. He leaves a wife and five children to mourn their loss.

Married, on the 15th inst., by Judge KEELIN COOK, MR. JOHN MCDONALD, to MISS JANE HARRIS, all of this city.

Died, in this city on the evening of the 15th inst., WILLIAM MONTGOMERY, youngest child of DR. JAMES M. GREEN, aged nineteen months.

Issue of March 29, 1853

Died, in this city on the 12th inst., PHILO EMMA, first and only child of JNO. S. and ELIZABETH ANN LIVINGSTON, aged six months and twelve days.

Married, in this city on Thursday evening, 31 ult., by the Rev. MR. E. QUIGLEY, MR. JOHN MALONE, to MISS CATHERINE CAVANNAH, all of this city.

Runaway – Was committed to the Jail of the city of Petersburg, Va. on the 24th day of August last, as a runaway slave, a negro man who says his name is GEORGE. He is about 26 or 27 years of age, 5 feet 2 ¼ inches high, (without shoes) dark brown complexion, stout built, tolerably likely, and has a large scar on the crown of the head, occasioned, (as he says) by a burn; he reads and writes well, and is a remarkably intelligent negro.

GEORGE now makes the following statement which varies a little from the one made when first committed: He says that he was purchased in Richmond, Virginia, about 12 years since, by MR. JAMES FURLOUGH, a Planter in Macon county, Georgia, who owned him some three years from whom he ran away so often that he sold him to his brother-in-law FRANKLIN BIBBINGS, in Sumter county, Georgia, with whom he lived about one year, ran away, was arrested and committed to the Jail in Macon, Bibb county, Georgia, who sold him out of Jail to ELIHU CRYSWILL, a trader in Macon, who owned him about one year and sold him to a MR. MOTT, who kept the Washington Hall in that place – that he in a short time sold him to a trader by the name of TROWBRIDGE living in Augusta – that he soon sold him to GARRET MARGERUM of Marietta, Georgia, who sold him to PATRICK ANDERSON of the same place – that MARGERUM and ANDERSON owned him about 15 months, and while he belonged to ANDERSON, he ran away in company with a boy named SAM, belonging to MR. JAMES L. SMITH, of Marietta – they were arrested and lodged in Jail in Lafayette, Walker county, Georgia, and were taken out by their respective owners, that ANDERSON sold him to a MR. CAZORT or KIZOT, a trader from Kentucky, who sold him in a short time to WILLIAM JONES, of Carrol county, Georgia, and then taken by JONES to Macon county, Alabama and sold to JOHN G. GOODE of said county, who moved to Montgomery county about 3 years ago, from whom he ran away in May last. He says that he is a first rate cook and was hired as such for about three months in 1851, to the proprietor of Montgomery Hall, Alabama. The owner is requested to come forward, prove property, pay charges and take him away or he will be disposed of on the third Thursday in June next: the laws of this state require him to be sold, and the money, after deducting legal expenses to be paid into the public treasury.

J. BRANCH, Sergeant
City Petersburg, Va.

Issue of April 12, 1853

Married, in Perry, Ga., on the 16th ultimo, by the Rev. E. P. BIRCH, MR. WM. M. ELDER, of Pike county to MISS ANN T. JOBSON, of the former place.

On the 5th instant, by the Rev. N. OUSLEY, MR. HENRY M. BAILEY, of this city, to MISS MARY A. GATES, of this county.

Obituary – Departed this life on the 4th ult., MR. GEORGE W. WARDLAW, aged about 36 years. The deceased was a native of Jones county, but had been for a number of years a resident of Houston. He was an honest man, honorable in all his deportment, a successful farmer, a good husband, father, neighbor and friend...He has left an affectionate wife; three small children, and numerous friends and relations to sorrow for their loss.

Issue of April 26, 1853

Death of the Vice - President. Most of our readers are, no doubt, already aware that the Hon. WM. R. KING, of Alabama, Vice-President of the United States, departed this life on Monday, the 18th instant.

He died full of years and full of honors. Born in April 1786, he lived to see the thirteen colonies of Great Britain expand into a glorious confederation of soverign States, which challenge the admiration of the world. At the early age of twenty-four years, MR. KING was chosen to represent North Carolina in the popular branch of Congress. Since that period, up to the time of his death, he was constantly engaged in offices of high honor and trust...

Issue of May 3, 1853

Fire – About five o'clock on the afternoon of Saturday last, the dwelling house of DR. JAMES M. GREEN, of this city, was discovered to be in flames and was soon reduced to ashes. The fire is supposed to have been communicated from one of the chimneys to the building. We understand that the house was nearly covered by insurance. Considerable loss was sustained, however, in the destruction of books, furniture, etc.

Incendiarism – We understand that an attempt was made to fire the premises of DR. JOHN B. WILEY on last Sunday night – a large bundle of inflammable matter being discovered under one corner of his residence.

Robbery – The house of the Reverend SYLVANUS LANDRUM, was entered last Saturday night and robbed of his watch, the halves of several hundred dollars, besides fifteen dollars in whole bills.

A Man Killed by His Wife – We regret to learn that on Sunday evening the 1st inst., WILEY HOFFMAN, of Emmanuel county, was killed by his wife. The facts, as we have them from a gentleman of that county, seem to be as follows: HOFFMAN had been at some of the neighboring dramshops during the day, and had become very much intoxicated; he started for home, and arrived late in the evening, he took his gun and shot a dog lying in the yard, at which his wife made some remarks, he then turned to her and commenced abusing and cursing her, swearing that he would kill her, and picked up his gun and attempted to shoot, she ran and he after her, he threw the gun at her, then took up a stake some eight or nine feet long, pursued her and coming up with her, knocked her down, after recovering enough to rise, he still thumping her, she drew a pistol and shot him in the heart, he then drew his knife, she ran again, and he after her, and continued the pursuit till he fell from exhaustion; he lived but a short while after he fell, but became more composed and sober before he died. Such is the statement we have of this sad transaction; the parties, it is said, have not lived very pleasantly together; HOFFMAN was a drinking man, and frequently in his cup.

MRS. HOFFMAN gave herself up to the officers, and after an examination before JAS. M. TAPLEY, a Justice of the Peace, was put under bonds for appearance at the Superior Court of that county.

Central Georgia

Death of JOHN A. STUART. We learn from Beaufort, that MR. JOHN A. STUART died on Tuesday, the 3d inst, aged 53 years. He was for a long time the proprietor and principal editor of this paper, but for nearly ten years, broken down both in body and mind, he as ceased to have any connection with the political affairs of the State.

Melancholy Occurrence – We learn that five negroes belonging to MR. JAMES POTTER were drowned last evening while attempting to cross the river to their quarters during the thunderstorm. There were seven negroes in the flat when it was struck by a squall of wind and upset. All but two of the party were drowned.

Savannah News

Married, in this city on Tuesday the 10th inst. by the Rev. MR. BROCK, MR. SAMUEL BOYKIN of Columbus to MISS LAURA J. daughter of the Hon. E. A. _____ of this place.

In Nashville (?) on Thursday the 12th inst., by the Rev. MR. SPEAR (?), DR. JOSEPH A. FLOURNOY, of Baker county to MISS ANNA, daughter of I. WINSHIP, Esq. of this city.

Issue of May 24, 1853

Two small wooden houses, near the Railroad Bridge in this city, were destroyed by fire, about 7 o'clock P.M. on Thursday last. The pecuniary loss was inconsiderable, but an old and infirm negro woman met a horrible death in the flames. The houses, as we are informed, were owned by D. DEMPSEY, Esq. of Macon.

Married, on the 17th instant, by the Rev. C. A. THARP, MR. HUGH L. DENARD, of Houston county, to MRS. FRANCES S. A. SOLOMON, of Twiggs county.

On Thursday evening, 12th instant, at the house of MRS. MARTHA STOVALL, in Crawford county, by C. H. WALKER, Esq. MR. WILLIAM RICKERSON to MISS MARTHA E. STOVALL.

Died, in this city, on the 12th instant, MR. WILLIAM SKELTON KING, aged about 35 years. MR. K. was a native of Richmond, Va. but had resided for several years in Charleston, S. C. previous to his removal to this city in February, 1849. Since that time, except when incapacitated by ill health, he has been Foreman of this office. He was buried with military honors by the Macon Volunteers of which corps he was a member, on the 14th inst.

Issue of May 31, 1853

A negro man named TOBE, attempted to kill MR. NATHAN HAWKINS, of Milledgeville, on Saturday night last. MR. HAWKINS, who is in feeble health had occasion to correct the wife of TOBE, in consequence of which the fellow attacked him, and attempted with a large knife to cut his throat. MR. HAWKINS was very badly hurt, as were also MRS. HAWKINS and her sister MRS. BAILY, who it is supposed went to the assistance of MR. H. The wounds of the ladies are not considered dangerous. TOBE and his wife are in jail.

Supposed Murder – Singular Affair – The Dodge county Gazette says: "Many of our readers will recollect that sometime last November we published an account of the finding of the body of a man in the town of Ashippun, this county, supposed at that time to have committed suicide, and that was the decision of the Coroner. It is now supposed the man was murdered. The facts in the case, as we learned them from a neighbor of the deceased, are as follows: 'A young man by the name of EDWIN BUNDA, formerly of Oswego, in the State of N. York, where his father now resides, had been living for two or three years previous to his disappearance, in Ashippun, and was paying his addresses to the daughter of HIRAM SANDERS, also of Ashippun. The father, (H.S.) had forbid young BUNDA from coming to his house and having anything to say to his daughter, and threatened, if he persisted in coming, to make way with him.'

' The young man continued to visit the daughter, and it is supposed, in the latter part of June last, went to invite her to attend a ball, since which time he has not been seen alive. SANDERS was arrested as being the murderer, and is now in jail at this place, awaiting his trial at the next term of the Circuit Court, which met on the 23d instant. The father of the young man has recently come from Oswego to investigate the matter, and says the remains of the man found are those of his son. He recognizes him from his teeth, which were very peculiar and different from common teeth – also from some of his clothing. MISS SANDERS died about four weeks ago in consequence of the supposed murder of her intended.'

A Singular and Affecting Incident – It is stated that MRS. NEWALL, the mother of DAVID B. NEWALL, of Newport, N. H., who was killed on board the New Haven cars at Norwalk, did not hear of her son's death until Wednesday of last week. He was a consumptive young man, and had been to the South. His mother proceeded as far as Georgia to accompany him home, but he passed her on the road without knowing it. She started on her return, and being a stranger held no conversation with anyone. On Wednesday she took the New York and New Haven train, when a gentleman handed her a newspaper which contained an account of the Norwalk massacre. She immediately commenced reading a list of those killed, when suddenly she dropped the paper, and raising her hands, exclaimed, "My God! My God! My son is killed!" This was her first intimation of her bereavement, and her son had already arrived at home and been consigned to the grave.

Issue of June 7, 1853

Death of Captain SCOTT – Captain ALEXANDER SCOTT, a well known and highly respected resident of Macon, died suddenly in New York, upon Wednesday, the 1st of June.

Capt. SCOTT was about 40 years of age, and at the time of his death, was one of the proprietors of the Lanier House of this city. Although a native of Maryland, he had resided in Georgia for fifteen years, and was widely known as a man of great public spirit, and rare energy of character. He received a Captain's commission in the 13th Infantry during the Mexican War, though he was prevented by ill health from taking an active part in the campaign.

From the Charleston Courier – Married on Tuesday evening, May 31st, by the Rev. PAUL TRAPIER KEITH, DONALD G. MITCHELL, of Connecticut, to MARY F., daughter of WM. B. PRINGLE, of this city.

Died, near Hopewell, Crawford co., Ga., on Thursday, 26th inst., REBECCA JULIA, only daughter of WM. T. and MARTHA A. NORTHEN, aged 17 months, 1 day.

Issue of June 14, 1853

Died, at Americus, Ga. on Sunday evening, June 5th, ARTHUR DAVIS, infant son of ELIZA M. and Rev. P. A. STROBEL, aged 13 days.

Issue of June 21, 1853

Death of Rev. SAMUEL J. CASSELLS. This gentleman, who was for many years the officiating Clergyman of the Presbyterian church in this city, died in Savannah, a few days since, after a long and painful illness.

Issue of June 28, 1853

Died, on the 1st instant, MR. THOMAS WINN, in the 88th year of his age.

Died on the 22d of May last, FRANCIS HOGE, second (?) son of JOHN S. and LOUISA A. HOGE, aged 3 years.

Fifty Dollars Reward – Ranaway from the subscriber in Macon, Ga., in October last, a negro girl named FRANCES or FANNY, about 20 years old, of a copper complexion, very likely, she has probably been decoyed off by some white person. I will give fifty dollars reward for the delivery of the girl in some safe jail, where I can get her, and the apprehension of the person harboring her, with proof to convict him; or I will give twenty-five dollars for the delivery of the girl to me in Macon or in any safe jail.

DAVID JAMESON

Issue of July 5, 1853

$1050 Reward –I will pay One Thousand Dollars for evidence to convict any white person of harboring my Negro man RICHARD, who has absconded, and Fifty Dollars for his arrest, so I can get him.

S. T. BAILEY

Issue of July 12, 1853

We regret to learn that an accident occurred in working the steam shovel on the Augusta and Waynesboro Road, by which Gen. T. J. WARTHEN, had two of his best negroes, seriously, if not fatally injured.

Married, on the 5th instant, by the Rev. CARY COX, Maj. EDWIN HARRIS, of Montgomery, Macon county, Ga., to MISS SARAH ELIZABETH, only daughter of D. R. ANDREWS, Esq., of Stanfordville, Ga.

Obituary –Died at the residence of her mother, in Knoxville, Crawford county, on Tuesday morning, 5th instant, MISS MARY W. SLATTER, daughter of LEMNEL D. SLATTER, late of said county deceased, in her 16th year.

Died, in this city, on the 2d instant, DR. ELLIOT J. SMITH, aged 27 years.

$50 Reward – Ranaway from the subscriber on the night of the 25th ultimo, Houston county, Georgia, a negro man named JOHN, about 23 years old, and about five feet six or seven inches high, of yellow complexion, and rather yellowish eyes, a carpenter by trade. It is very likely he was decoyed off by a white man by the name of JAMES FOSTER, as he was discovered lying around the plantation two or three days previous to the time the boy left, and had several talks with the boy during the time.
I will give Fifty Dollars Reward for the delivery of the boy in some safe jail so I can get him, and the apprehension of the person harboring him, with proof to convict him; or I will give Twenty-five Dollars for the delivery of the boy to me, about ten miles East of Oglethorpe.

Issue of July 19, 1853

MR. MAURICE O'CONNELL, M. P. the eldest son of the great DANIEL O'CONNELL, died suddenly on the 17th June, at his apartments, in London.

Issue of July 26, 1853

MISS LAURA SHIELDS, who resided on Liberty street, went up to her room on the evening of July 4th, to dress for a ball to be given at Union Hall, on Broadway. When the gentleman came who was to accompany her, she had not come downstairs. Her mother called her, but she did not come, though nearly an hour passed in waiting for her. At length her mother went to the door and rapped, but no answer was returned, and she had locked the door.

They then became alarmed and forced the door, when LAURA was found lying upon the floor nearly dressed for

131

the ball, and dead. She appeared to be in perfect health in the evening at ten. She was buried in the dress they found her in, on Monday.
Cincinnati Gazette

MR. FRANCIS COOLEY was instantly killed by lightning on Tuesday of last week at Peoria, Wycoming county, New York. The deceased was attending in his store, felling a camphene can, when the lightning entered at the back of the building, struck him near the head, and passed out through his heel, entirely stripping him of his clothes and causing instant death. The camphene was also inflamed, and when MRS. COOLEY entered the room, hardly a moment having elapsed, the deceased was standing upright against the wall, enveloped in a sheet of flame. MRS. COOLEY and her sister were sitting, at the time, about a table, in a room over the store, and the top of the table was separated from its legs in an instant. Two persons were in the store at the time – one a young man standing near the door was tossed into the street, a distance of nearly twenty feet – the other, a lady, was prostrated and rendered senseless but neither was seriously injured.

Married, on the 14th instant, by the Hon. JOSEPH DAY, DR. JAMES F. BARRON, of Clinton, Ga., to MISS JOANNA E., daughter of JAMES W. and MARTHA SHROPSHIRE of Jasper county.

Died, at the residence of his brother-in-law, G. M. DUNCAN, Esq., in Dooly county, Ga. on the night of the 11th (?) instant, DANIEL W. SHINE, Jr., in the ____year of his age.

Died, at her residence, near this city, on the 24th ___, MRS. SARAH HUGHES, in the 65th (?) year of her age.

Issue of August 9, 1853

Died, near Bateman's Store, in Houston county, on the 15th ult., of inflammation of the lungs, MRS. SICY BROOKINGS, in the 41st year of her age. MRS. B. was born in Washington county, Ga., but for the last four years a resident of Houston county. She was a member of the Baptist Church for the last 12 years and has left a husband and three children to mourn their irreparable loss.

Issue of August 16, 1853

Married, near Hawkinsville, Ga., on the 4th inst., by Judge S. M. MANNING, HENRY H. WHITFIELD, Esq. to MISS ELIZABETH J. PIPKIN, daughter of Judge ASA PIPKIN.

On the 10th instant, by the Rev. R. C. SMITH, MR. G. W. ROSS, of Baldwin, to MISS SAVANNAH CARTER, of Putnam county, Ga.

Died, at the Floyd House, in the city of Macon, on the evening of the 6th instant, N. G. SLAUGHTER, Esq., of Marion county, Ga. He was taken with diarrhea, on a visit to the city of Brunswick and had got this far on his return home, when he became so feeble, as to be forced to stop. He lingered here for ten days, suffering great pain. His death was very easy and in full hope of blessed immortality.

At his residence in Oglethorpe, on the 27th ult., DR. JAMES M. FOKES, aged about 31 years. The deceased was formerly a resident of Jefferson county.

Death while on the way to the altar – A young man by the name of EDMUND SLATTENLY, while on his way from Franklin to Milford, on Sunday week, to be married, met with a singular and fatal accident. He stopped at a well to water his horse, when the bucket fell into the well. He descended to obtain it, when the wall caved in and buried him. He was a native of Ireland. His intended wife accompanying him on the journey, when this singular death thus intervened to destroy their bright anticipations. Woosochet Patriot

Ranaway from the subscriber, living in Pulaski county, near Hawkinsville, on the 31st of July, 1853, a negro man by the name of HAWKINS, he is of medium height and of a yellow complexion, it is said that he is half Indian, and may probably have a pass with him, but not given by me; he has a white spot in one of his eyes and speaks very positive when spoken to; he weighs about 150 pounds. The boy was bought from a trader by the name of JOHN CROUCH; he was brought from the upper part of North Carolina and I think he will try to make his way back there. I will give a liberal reward for him or his confinement in any safe jail so that I can get him.

DAVID LINDSEY

Issue of August 23, 1853

$50 Reward – Ranaway from the subscriber on the night of the 25th ultimo, Houston county, Georgia, a Negro man named JOHN, about 23 years old, and about five feet six or seven inches high, of yellow complexion, and rather yellowish eyes, a carpenter by trade. It is very likely he was decoyed off by a white man by the name of JAMES FOSTER, as he was discovered lying around the plantation two or three days previous to the time the boy left, and had several talks with the boy during the time.

I will give Fifty Dollars Reward for the delivery of the boy in some safe jail so I can get him, and the apprehension of the person harboring him, with proof to convict him I will ____ ____five dollars ____

The delivery of the boy to me, about ten miles East of Oglethorpe.

WILLIAM WEST

Issue of August 30, 1853

The Recent S. Carolina Duel – We published a telegraphic dispatch some days since, announcing a fatal duel at Charleston, the papers of which city have been silent as to the nature of the difficulty. The Washington Star, of Saturday, however, gives the following particulars: MR. LEGARE was engaged to a young lady in Columbia. Her friends inquired of DUNOVANT what was the character and habits of L.? This coming to his ears, he inquired of D. what he had answered; and found that he had spoken favorably of him. But not satisfied with a verbal statement, he demanded it in writing, which was refused. LEGARE challenged on this refusal. The distance was 12 paces. LEGARE fired at the word "one" and missed; DUNOVANT fired at the word "two" and killed his antagonist. The survivor was wholly unskilled in the use of the pistol, having never before had anything to do with a

135

duel. LEGARE, on the contrary, was notoriously, a crack shot, having, a few days before the affair come off, in practicing, placed 48 out of 50 balls in a card at the word. He became very nervous on starting for the ground, and remarked that he felt a presentment that he would fall, notwithstanding his skill with the pistol. He was formerly in the Navy, as a Midshipman, from which he was dismissed, it is said, for running a sword through a marine."

On Hundred Dollars Reward – Ranaway from the subscriber, Pulaski county, Georgia, on the 18th July, a negro man named HENRY, about twenty-three or four years old, and about five feet five or six inches high, of black complexion. Speaks quick when spoken to, and has but little to say to any persons. Also his brother ELI, which ranaway sometime in December last; he is about five feet high, rather light complected, and about twenty years old. I will pay the above reward for the delivery of the boys to me or in any safe Jail, so I can get them; or I will pay fifty dollars for the delivery of either.

JAMES M. MCCOMICK

Issue of September 6, 1853

JOAQUIN captured, beheaded, and his head in the hands of his captors - It has been reported here that the company of Rangers, commanded by Captain HARRY LOVE, met with the notorious murderer and robber. JOAQUIN, and six of his equally infamous band, at Panocha Pass, and after a desparate running fight, JOAQUIN and one of his gang were killed and two taken prisoners; three managed to make their escape, but one of their horses was killed and several captured. Captain LOVE is now on his way down with his prisoners and the head of JOAQUIN presented in spirits. One of LOVE'S company was seriously injured.

T. A. C.

Died – In this city, on the 30th ult., BENJAMIN PORT (or FORT), in the fiftieth year of his age. For many years a resident of Middle Georgia. He will long live in the memory of his friends.

In Pond Town, Georgia, on the 30th ult., NANCY BASS, daughter of Dr. A. B. and MRS. R. H. GREENE, aged 3 years and 2 days.

Dishonest Act – A Great Mistake by a Bank Teller HENRY ROSENTHAL, a German, living at 87 Allen street, on Wednesday morning, having a check for $9.12 on the Hanover Bank, proceeded to that institution and presented the check for payment to E. B. COBB, Esq. the Paying Teller. The latter having a great deal of business on hand at that moment, glanced hastily at the check, and forthwith handed MR. ROSENTHAL the sum of $912 instead of 9.12, which ROSENTHAL gathered up and left the Bank. In the afternoon, MR. COBB, in arranging his accounts, ascertained that there was a large deficiency of cash, for which he was puzzled to account. In order to ascertain the truth of the matter, MR. COBB compared checks with the check clerk, and at once discovered that he had, by accident, paid ROSENTHAL $912 instead of $9.12, the amount for which the check was drawn. ROSENTHAL on being arrested denied all knowledge of the whole matter. Officer MASTERSON, however, was not to be put off with this denial but proceeded to search his truck, where he found eight hundred dollar bills, which discovery brought ROSENTHAL to terms. He then admitted receiving the money and said he would make it all right. His person was then searched, which resulted in finding more money, in fact nearly the amount dishonestly appropriated. ROSENTHAL was committed to await examination on a charge of constructive larceny.

From a card found in possession of ROSENTHAL, it appears he is a commission merchant, doing business at No. 135 Broadway, where he deals in all varieties of fancy goods, German and Havanna cigars. The same card also shows that he is an agent for the firm of Sherbert & Co.
New York Herald

Issue of September 13, 1853

$1050 Reward – I will pay One Thousand Dollars for evidence to convict any white person of harboring my Negro man RICHARD, who has absconded, and Fifty Dollars for his arrest, so I can get him.

S. T. BAILEY

Terrible Accident upon the Central Rail Road – An unfortunate man, by the name of DONAHOE, came to his death on the Central Railroad, on last Saturday night, under the following painful circumstances: In consequence of the late heavy rains, one of the abutments of the Bridge, crossing Walnut Creek, had become very insecure, and at the first pressure of the engine, sunk from eight to ten inches. The engine being thus thrown off the track, drew the train along the timbers of the bridge, several of which penetrated the cars, and one of them crushed DONOHOE in a most horrible manner – His hips, thighs and spine were awfully mangled – so terribly, that although he survived the accident about two hours, he is said to have experienced little if any pain. The unfortunate man was an Irishman by birth, and was on his road to Macon, for the purpose of taking the place of head waiter at the Lanier House. He was buried in this city on Sunday afternoon with the ceremonies of the Roman Catholic Church.

Death of Com. JOSIAH TATTNALL, U. S. N. The Washington Star, says: "We regret to have to write that a telegraphic dispatch was received at New York on Saturday, from Pensacola, saying that Commodore TATTNALL, (the commander of the yard there,) whose alarming illness we announced on Thursday last, was dead, and that the virulence of the fever was such as to have compelled the remaining authorities to close the Pensacola Navy Yard, and move all hands some distance up the river."

Commodore TATTNALL was native Georgian, son of JOSIAH TATTNALL, formerly Governor of this State, and was at the time of his death, about 55 or 60 years of age...He was at the repulse of the British at Craney Island, in 1812, and was afterwards at the battle of Bladensburgh; and during the late war with Mexico he was commander of "Musquito Fleet"; under the walls of Vera Cruz. On all occasions he conducted himself with bravery and gallantry. Commodore TATTNALL leaves many friends and acquaintances in this city...We presume that his remains will be brought to this city, and will find their last resting place in the family vault of the TATTNALLS, at Bonaventure, four miles South of this city. Sav. Republican

Mutiny on board the Ship France – Boston Sept. 3 – The bark Cuba, Captain HOWE, from Palermo, arrived at this

139

port yesterday afternoon, having on board in irons, JOHN DUDLEY, one of the crew of the ship France, Capt. TEAL, charged with three others, with making a murderous attack upon Capt. TEAL, on the 26th July last on board said ship.

The France belongs to Philadelphia, and is now on her trip from Pernambuco, bound for New York, with three of her crew in irons, jointly charged with DUDLEY. During the melee, Capt. TEAL, was struck with an axe, and severely wounded.

The second mate, JAMES KNIGHT, was shot with a pistol, the ball lodging in his shoulder from whence it was subsequently extracted, and at last accounts KNIGHT was doing well. DUDLEY has been committed to jail for examination.

Charge of Fraud – New York, September 5. A man named GUTMAN, well known here, and engaged for a long time as customer broker in this city, enjoying the full confidence of a large portion of foreign importing houses, disappeared on last Thursday morning and has not since been heard of. He is said to be a defaulter to the Union Bank for about one hundred thousand dollars. Also, to Messrs. Spies, Chust & Co., and several others, amounts varying from $5,000 to 10,000 each. He has left a wife and large family of children in this city. The presumption is that he has gone to Europe.

Married – In Bibb county, on the 28th ult., by the Hon. JOHN H. BRANTLY, MR. ROBERT H. LODGE, to MISS MARY E. WILLIAMS.

In Americus, on the 31st ult., Dr. JOSEPH MCDONALD, of this city, to MISS HARRIET A. FOSTER.

Died – In Crawford county, on the 3d instant, after a severe attack of Typhoid Fever, FREDERICK HARDISON, Esq., in the 74th year of his age. MR. HARDISON was born and raised in Washington county, North Carolina, but a resident of the county of Crawford for the last twenty-nine years. He has left an aged wife and several children to mourn...

A telegraphic dispatch from Buffalo published in the New York papers of the 8th says that SUCED alias WATSON, the negro recently arrested at Niagara, charged with the murder of JAMES E. JONES, of this place, was on Thursday morning last discharged from custody by Judge SHELDON, of Buffalo, on the ground that the man was a fugitive slave, and there were no papers to detain him.

Savannah Georgian

The death of ex-Senator POINDEXTER is announced. He was the first representative of Mississippi when a territory, and subsequently one of her U. S. Senators. He was a member of the Senate in the trying times of Gen. JACKSON'S administration and, with WEBSTER, CLAY CALHOUN, SPAGUE, HOLMES, and others, made some of the most brilliant Phillippies(?) then directed against that administration, which he had at first supported. He was a very able man and a fierce hater, and he made his mark in every position he occupied. We believe he was born in Kentucky. He was in this city a long time in 1841; at the head of the committee appointed by the President to investigate affairs of the New York Custom House. New York Express, 7th Inst.

Dreadful Accident on the Steamer Bay-State. About half-past three o'clock this morning while the steamer Bay-State, Capt. W. M. BROWN was on her way through the Sound, from Fall River to this port, and when off Black Rock, about six miles this side of Bridgeport, Ct., one of her crank pins broke – The consequence was that, at the next evolution, the head of the cylinder was knocked off and the steam escaped with great force.

Most of the passengers were in the state rooms, and if they had remained there would probably have been uninjured, but hearing the crash of the breaking machinery, and the noise of the escaping steam, they were naturally much alarmed, and ran into the saloons to ascertain the danger and seek some means of escape. Hence a number were scalded more or less severely, although fortunately none were instantly killed.

The steamer Connecticut, from Norwich, took the passengers from the Bay State, and brought them to New York. On arriving here, it was deemed advisable to take the following persons to the city hospital: MISS CHARLOTTE SNOW, of Dartsmouth, Mass, MR. THOMAS WARNER, of Dartsmouth, Mass., ANN ELIZA DE WOLF, aged 16, CHARLOTTE DE WOLF, aged 14, MARY DE WOLF aged 10, MARIA DE WOLF aged 8 (children of MR. WM. F. DEWOLF of Chicago, Ill.) MISS SNOW is scalded badly on the arms, and less severely on the face, but the rest of her person is uninjured. She suffers little pain, and is in no apparent danger. MR. WARNER is very seriously scalded externally, and it is feared internally, although his medical attendant has not yet expressed a decided opinion.

The four children of MR. DE WOLF are also very badly scalded – two of them, it is feared, fatally. Their father, who escaped injury, is in attendance upon them at the hospital. It is probable that several scalded persons have been carried to their hotels or private residences; but the above are the only names we have been able to ascertain.

No blame is attached to the officers of the Bay State. The accident seems to have been unavoidable and when it occurred they did all in their power to alleviate the distress of the passengers.

Since the foregoing account was put to type we have received the following additional information: MR. WILSON, of Water street, New York and MISS WILSON, his daughter, were badly scalded.

MISS HAVEN, of Fall River, hands terribly scalded.

MR. J. E. ABBOTT, of Boston, had his two hands scalded, so as to destroy the use of each.

New York Commercial, 8th

Obituary – Died at the residence of her mother in Bibb county, on Saturday, the 10th day of September, 1853, after an attack for twenty-two days of typhoid fever, MISS MARTHA A. JONES (?)

Died in Athens, on the 17th ult., EDWARD _____, youngest son of JOHN J. and MARY E. GRAHAM (?) aged one year and seven months.

In Barnesville, Ga., on 20th August, W. M. DUMAS, son of DAVID S. & C. B. DINNAS, aged_____months and 29 days.

Death of Capt. P. WILTBERGER – Although not altogether an unexpected event, we regret to have to announce today the death of Capt. P. WILTBERGER, of this city, which occurred at the Mansion House, in Brooklyn, at four o'clock P.M. on Thursday last...
Capt. WILTBERGER was born in Philadelphia and at the time of his decease, was about sixty-two years of age. In his earliest years, he was a sea captain, connected with the China trade; then removed to Georgia, and settled in East Macon; thence, coming to Savannah he was commander for several years, on the line of steamers plying between this city and Augusta and Charleston. Afterwards, for a time, a merchant doing business in Savannah; and next, proprietor of the City Hotel, from which he retired to become the host of the Pualski House, which he first rented, and finally, by prudent management and perservering industry, was enabled to buy; and of which _____establishment he was the popular proprietor to the day of his demise.

Savannah Georgian

Capt. INGRAHAM – Commander DUNCAN H. INGRAHAM is the son of the late NATHANIEL INGRAHAM, of Charleston, S. C. Almost all his ancestors have been in some way connected with naval affairs. His father was as intimate friend of Capt. PAUL JONES, and volunteered under him on the first cruise of the Bonhomme Richard in 1779, and was in the desperate action with the British frigate Serapis. His uncle, Capt. JOS. INGRAHAM, U.S.N. was lost on board the U.S. Ship Pickering, which was lost at sea and never heard from afterward. His cousin, WM. INGRAHAM, a lieutenant in the Navy, was killed at the age of 20. Capt. INGRAHAM married HARRIET R. LAURENS, of South Carolina, granddaughter of HENRY LAURENS, President of the First Continental Congress, who was captured and confined for a long time in the Tower of London. It is a curious fact, that by intermarriage of his progenitors, Captain INGRAHAM is related to some of the most distinguished officers in the British Navy, among whom we name Capt. MARRAYATT, C.B., now in command of the Arctic Expedition. Norfolk Herald

Married – At the house of DAVID BOWERS, on Sunday morning 18th inst., by CHARLES H. WALKER, Esq., MR. RICHARD YARBROUGH. To MISS EPSY ANN GRAY, all of Crawford county.

Obituary – Died, in this city, on Sunday evening, 18th instant, MRS. MARTHA J. A. BURNHAM, wife of WILLIAM C. BURNHAM, and second daughter of JOHN P. and R. A. EVANS, in her 23d year.

Died, in the 53d year of her age, at the residence of her husband near this city, MRS. LYDIA RICHARDSON, wife of JAMES RICHARDSON. The deceased was a native of South Carolina, but for many years had resided in and near this city. How well in her retired sphere of life she performed the duties of neighbor, wife and mother, is attended by the regrets of her many friends, and the grief of her bereaved husband and surviving children.

Issue of October 11, 1853

Death of WM. W. WIGGINS, Esq. – It is with great sorrow that we chronicle the demise of WM. W. WIGGINS, Esq. who breathed his last in Griffin on Thursday night last. MR. WIGGINS was a member of the Georgia Legislature, and was prominently identified with the recent legislation of the State – having been a prominent advocate of the ad valorem tax law, and have been connected with various other legal reforms whose salutary influence is generally acknowledged. He was possessed of many amiable and sterling qualities and in his death the State loses a faithful servant.

Fatal Accident from Burning Fluid – MRS. SUSAN SWEENEY, the mother of several children was burned to death in Philadelphia on Monday night, in consequence of a fluid lamp taking fire and communicating the flame to her dress. In New York, on Saturday night a can of the extract of Orange exploded in a drug store, by which a girl named ELIZABETH NEVIN, was so horribly burned as to cause her instant death. ANN E. TORVILL was badly burned at the same time. They were pouring it into another can, when the vapor arising from it came in contact with the flame of a lamp, and explosion ensued.

Tribute of Respect – On the third day of the term, the Hon. JAMES J. SCARBOROUGH announced to the court the death of the Hon. ANGUS. M. D. KING...

Marriage and Death notices difficult to read.

Runaway – From the subscriber, in Macon, Georgia, on the second day of September, a negro boy by the name of

DAVE, of a bright dark complexion, inclined to be bow-legged, about 5 feet 7 or 8 inches high. Said boy belongs to Hon. W.W. MANGHAM, of N. C. and is either making his way back or working by the job with a forged pass.
A reasonable reward will be paid for his apprehension.

EDWARD MORIARTY

Issue of October 18, 1853

Runaway – On the 8th instant, my negro man STERLING, he is about 28 years old, about 6 feet high, of dark complexion, one of his middle fingers is stiff, caused by being mashed. I expect he is strolling about the city, or he is gone in the country somewhere. I will give a liberal reward to any person that will deliver him to me, or _____him in some jail so I can get him. I bought him from MR. R. BUNN, about 18 months ago.

JAMES WILLIAMS

Homicide – A private letter to the Mobile Advertiser, dated the 1st inst., says: CHARLES WINTERS was killed this morning by A. J. COLLINS. They had some few words together, when COLLINS drew a pistol, fired at CHARLEY, who was then standing in his door, and COLLINS in the street, but he missed him. CHARLEY then sprang towards him. COLLINS, who had a sword cane, drew the sword, made a lunge and ran him through, entering the abdomen about three inches below the navel. He did not live more than half an hour after he was stabbed. COLLINS is in jail. Great excitement in town, as you may well imagine.

Brutal Murder – A man named SULLIVAN brutally murdered his wife at Fort Hamilton, N. Y. on Tuesday, because, through weakness from recent confinement, she

146

let a box of coal, which he compelled her to assist him to lift, fall on his foot. He was arrested.

Issue of October 25, 1853

A letter has been received from Tampa, from which we learn that Gen. THOMAS CHILDS, of the U. S. Army, died at that place on the 8th inst., of yellow fever after an illness of four days.   Florida News

Gov. SEYMOUR , of New York, has offered a reward of one thousand dollars for the apprehension of the person or persons who violated and murdered a girl thirteen years of age, named CATHERINE QUIGLEY, near Jamaica, L. I. Last Sunday night. The citizens of Jamaica have offered a reward also, of five hundred dollars. The offenders are supposed to be black men.

Died – At his residence, in Dooly county, Ga. on the 27th August, 1853, after a lingering attack of congestive fever, ABNER HOLLIDAY, in the 88th (?) year of his age. The early (?) associates of MR. HOLLIDAY were identified with the scenes of the Revolutionary War in South Carolina, in which he took a patriotic stand in defence of the colonies. Soon after the close of the war, he removed to Georgia, where he has ever since resided...

Married – In Dooly county, on Thursday evening, 20th instant, by Rev. LIPSEY,MR. B___ M. GILES, of Montezuma, to MISS HILARY M., daughter of PORTLOCK (?) and ELIZA THOMPSON.

Elopement Extraordinary – Day before yesterday evening, officers HAZEN, RIDER and ROSE received a dispatch from Columbus, telling them to look out on the ten o'clock eastern train, for the parties in an elopement which had taken place from Hancock county.

147

The lady in the case was named DEER and the male individual concerned called JOHN CURTIS. The parties arrived as expected, and were taken into custody. The baggage was extensive, consisting of a band box, two carpet sacks, two trunks, a baby two months old, three hundred dollars of the deserted husband's money, and a six-shooter. The latter instrument was in the pocket of the lady, who drew it, and informed the officers that she would speedily cause vacancies in the organization of the Cincinnati police. She was secured and taken to the watch house, however, where she was lodged during the night. In the morning, her husband and her father arrived – the former to claim his baby, and the latter his erring daughter. Both, after a world of argument, were successful, and CURTIS was turned loose upon the world, unencumbered with baggage. Cin. Com.

Issue of November 1, 1853

The Late Duel at Charleston – The Courier of yesterday says: The case of the State vs. JOHN DUNOVANT, JR. arising out of the late duel, which resulted in the death of MR. JAMES D. LEGARE, was committed to the Grand Jury, on an indictment for murder, under a charge from his Honor Judge FROST; and the Jury, after examining witnesses, returned with finding "No Bill".

Died – In this city, on the 28th ult., JOSEPH FRANCIS, youngest child of JOSEPH and MARY KENNELLY, aged thirteen months.

In this city, on the morning of the 25th last, at 7 o'clock, MRS. LAURIE MASON, wife of M. M. MASON, aged ____ years.

Issue of November 8, 1853

Man and Horses Drowned – We learn on Tuesday last, a man by the name of WILLIAM CAMPBELL, employed in hauling lumber, drove to the ferry at the Railroad Bridge near Oglethorpe, and demanded to be set across the River, just as the cars reached Montezuma. The ferryman objected, as he had orders to set no person over while the cars were likely to pass. CAMPBELL rushed his team into the Flat, and being intoxicated whipped them severely to make them still. Stung by the lash, the horses jumped overboard. CAMPBELL was in the wagon, and was drawn over also, and they all perished. He formerly worked on the Railroad, and was about thirty-five years of age. The casualty was not produced by the noise of the Engine; for it occurred before the train left Montezuma for the bridge. Oglethorpe Democrat

Obituary – DONALD B. JONES, a resident of nearly forty years, died on the 18th September, after a protracted illness and suffering, in the 62nd year of his age...

Died – In this city on the 29th ult., CATHERINE VIRGINIA, daughter of THOMAS and CAROLINE RICHARDS, aged 6 years, 7 months and 7 days.

Issue of November 15, 1853

Married – On the 6th inst., by Rev. W. G. MCMICHAEL, DR. F. M. PITT of Indian Springs, Ga., to MISS REBECCA JORDAN (?) eldest daughter of Col B. F. WARD, of Butts county.

Died – On Saturday the 22d ult., of Congestion of the Brain, at the residence of his uncle, GARRETT SMITH in Houston county, WM. A. REDDING, aged 2 years 1 month and 1 week, eldest son of ABNER F. and A. E. REDDING.

Married – On the 1st instant, by the Rev. JOHN P. DUNCAN, MR. H. B. ELDER (?) of Barnesville, Pike county, Geo. To MISS SUSANNAH R. REDDING, daughter of Col. P. D. REDDING of Muscogee county, Ga.

Died – At Midway, near Milledgeville, on the 7th instant, MR. WM. T. BRYAN, aged 19 years, 6 months and 2 days, fourth son of DAVID and CATHERINE BRYAN, Bellview, Ga.

Near Oswich__, Russell county, Ala., on Monday the ____th instant, MR. STEPHEN EDWARDS, aged 65 years.

In Milledgeville, on the 4th instant, MRS. LAULA P. BEECHER, consort of S. T. BEECHER, Esq.

In Tuskegee, Alabama, on 21st October, 1853, SAMUEL B. DEN_E, a native of Schenectaday, N. Y., but for the last 34 years a resident of the South, aged 55 years, a coach painter by trade.

Issue of November 29, 1853

Death of THOMAS KING, SENIOR. It will be seen by reference to our Obituary Notices, that it has become our painful duty to record the death of one of our oldest and most esteemed citizens. MR. KING was a native of McIntosh county in this State – which county he represented for several years in the Legislature – besides holding other offices in the gift of its citizens. For the last twenty years, however, MR. K. has been a resident of this city and county, but for a great part of that time, has been confined to his house, by a most painful and uncontrollable disease. His sufferings, which frequently were of the most acute character, were with the firmness of a stoic and the resignation of a Christian...

Died – At his residence in this county, on the evening of the 23d, THOMAS KING, aged 65.

Issue of December 6, 1853

An Attempt To Murder – Four negroes, belonging to Col. JOSEPH A. L. LEE, of this county, attempted to murder MRS. LEE a few days since, in the absence of her husband. They had been administering a slow poison, but finding this ineffectual, they went to her room at night and had nearly succeeded in smothering, when she had presence of mind to arouse her little son by pinching him, whose outcry alarmed some faithful servants, who came to her rescue just in time to save her from a brutal death. The negroes have confessed their crime and are now in jail awaiting their trial. They do not impute their evil designs to any unkind treatment on the part of their mistress.

Columbus Times

W. R. O'NEAL was shot by some men by the name of BECK, near Beckville, in Carroll co., (Ga.) on the 13th. MR. O'NEAL is said to have received in his body seven balls and two loads of buckshot. He was still living at last accounts, though his situation was very dangerous.

Issue of December 13, 1853

Death of Col. R. A. L. ATKINSON – Another old citizen of Macon has been suddenly called from time into eternity! Col. ROBERT A. L. ATKINSON expired at his residence, in this city, last Wednesday morning, after a very brief and painful illness...Col. A. was a native of Jefferson county, bur for the last eight or ten years was an influential and highly respected citizen of this place...The immediate cause of this melancholy dispensation was an attack of erysipelas, which first exhibiting itself in the eyes, passed rapidly to the brain, and defied all medical treatment. Col. A. was probably about forty years of age…

Shocking Affair – Rev. GEO. W. CARAWAN, says the Wilmington Commercial of 2d instant, was tried before the Superior Court of Beaufort county, last week, in a case removed from Hyde, for the murder of a young man named LASSITOR, in November last, who had been teaching school near CARAWAN'S residence in Hyde. He was found guilty.
The North State Whig of Wednesday, says: "Just as the crowd commenced to leave, a report of a pistol was heard, followed immediately by another. CARAWAN had two self-cocking, single barrel pistols. With one he aimed at MR. WARREN. The ball struck just above his heart and glanced, making a slight wound. With the other he shot a hole through his own head. As we are going to press, he lies a corpse in the prisoner's box, a good part of his brain having run out upon the floor."
MR. WARREN was one of the council on the part of the State.

Issue of December 20, 1853

Another article on the death of ROBERT A. L. ATKINSON.

Married – In Americus, on the 13th inst., at the residence of _____, by the Rev. SAMUEL ANTHONY, DAVID R. ADAMS, Esq., to MRS. SARAH A. TRIPPE.

Issue of December 27, 1853

Attempted Highway Robbery and Murder – A daring outrage was perpetrated in the county of Philadelphia, on Wednesday evening last. As MR. ALEXANDER ERVIN, accompanied by his wife and little son, was driving home from Kensington, at about a quarter past nine o'clock, in a wagon drawn by one horse, he was suddenly startled, first by the appearance of two men, and then by the fact that one seized hold of his horse's head. The other leveled a pistol at MR. ERVIN, demanded his money, and threatened, in the event of his refusal, to blow his brains out. MR. E. said that he had no money, and the robber said that he knew better. At this the boy in the wagon attempted to strike the horse with a whip whereupon both the ruffians discharged their revolvers immediately into the wagon. The horse then started off at full speed, and could not be pulled up until he had gone more than a mile. MR. E. made a very narrow escape indeed. Two of the bullets passed immediately through his hat, and grazed the side and top of his head. His son was also wounded by a slug in the arm, while the outside of his coat was perforated with shot in twelve places. MRS. E. was not touched. The villains immediately after the horse sprang forward, ran across a lot towards Richmond and made their escape. They were apparently young – say about twenty-one years of age – Both wore caps of dark cloth. The outrage was committed about fifteen yards on this side of Gunner's Run. The moon was shining brightly at the time.

Phil. Enquirer

Riot on the Illinois Central Railroad – Chicago, Dec. 16 – A bloody riot took place among the laborers on the Illinois Central Railroad, at Lasalle, yesterday, growing out of a reduction of their wages.

About two o'clock an altercation arose between ALBERT STORY, a Contractor, and a party of Irishmen, during which one of the latter was shot dead. Shortly afterwards STORY's office was attacked and pillaged; and STORY who had concealed himself in a barn, was found and brutally murdered, his head and body being horribly mangled. MRS. STORY was also fired at, by escaped.

It is reported that MR. DUNN, STORY's foreman on the other side of the river, has shot 9 laborers.

The Sheriff of Lasalle county was speedily on the spot, and after some resistance, during which one Irishman was shot dead, and two wounded, thirty of the rioters were taken. The ringleader of the rioters has escaped, but measures have been taken for his apprehension.

Singular Accident – DR. AINSWORTH, who resides at No. 28 Somerset street, had his arm broken yesterday in rather a singular manner. He was reclining on a couch with a book in one hand, when the ringing of the door bell suddenly aroused him, and in attempting to arise, he broke his arm short off between the elbow and shoulder. The broken bone was set by a brother physician, and the doctor is now doing well.　　　　Boston Traveler

Suicide of a Georgian at Marshall, Texas. We learn from the Marshall Republican that a gentleman named WM. R. MOSS, from Hancock county, Ga., committed suicide in the house of DR. JOSEPH TAYLOR, in that place, on the night of the 2_th ult., by cutting his throat with a razor. He appears to have been, for some time previously, in a state of great nervous excitement. His effects were examined and found to amount in the aggregate to about $16,000 (?). The Republican says: An inquest was held over his body, and the verdict was rendered, "came to his death by his own hand." We understand that MR. MOSS has a mother and sister on the road to Texas with 120 negroes, of which 40 belonged to him.

DR. TAYLOR has delivered up the means of MR. MOSS, to two responsible gentlemen in this place for safe keeping, for which he holds their receip.

Married – On the 20th inst., by the Rev. S. ANTHONY, ROBERT N. BAILEY of Bibb county, to MISS LOUISE M., daughter of Rev. THOMAS BATTLE of Monroe county.

On the 20th inst., at the residence of her father, MR. GEORGE R. TURPIN, of this city, to MISS ELIZABETH, daughter of GREEN G. GUNN of Jones county.

On the 22d inst., at the residence of JOEL GRITLIN, Esq., in Oglethorpe, MR. JAMES W. GREEN of East Macon, to MISS EMILY BOYLE of Jones county.

In Athens, on Wednesday evening, the 21st inst., by the Rev. N. HOYT, D.D. ROBERT T. MCCAY, of Rome, to MISS SUSAN L. WILEY of Athens.

A Fortunate Editor – a gentleman of the Savannah press came down here, the other day, captured one of Leon County's fairest daughters and, we are told, will actually carry her off with him. As the affair has now become a matter of notoriety, we may as well give names. The editor we allude to is no less a person than R. B. HILTON, Esq., once our foreman of the Floridian, but now the accomplished conductor of the Savannah Georgian. The fair captive whom this unfeeling man has actually tied (with the silken cords of matrimony) is MISS REBECCA B. BRADFORD, daughter of Dr. EDWARD BRADFORD, of this county.
Well, we forgive MR. HILTON his sins against us, which are many; and wish him and his beautiful bride all the happiness two congenial souls may enjoy during a long life of mutual love and devotion.

Florida Sentinal

A Novel Marriage Ceremony – The Rev. MISS ANTOINETTE L. BROWN, this morning, as the officiating Clergyman, united a happy couple in the bonds of holy wedlock – thus probably becoming the pioneer in this interesting department of Women's Rights. The parties were DELOS ALLEN and ELIZA W. DEGARMO, both member of the Society of Friends. Those present state that the Rev. ANTOINETTE went through with the ceremony with marked grace and propriety. This is a progressive age — when man can be married by a girl as well as to a girl, and when girl doctors and girl divines undertake the cure of both body and soul.

Rochester Union

INDEX

A

165

167

D

173

175

M

188

T

199

201

W

About The Author

Newton Wilcox was born in Rome, Georgia. He graduated from Darlington School and Shorter College in Rome with a BA in History. He is a 7th grade Social Studies teacher in Columbia County, Georgia. He lives in Thomson, Georgia. This is his first book.